FEMALE TYCOONS

Rosemary Burr

ROSTERS LTD, LONDON

Designed and published by ROSTERS
Typeset by Gwynne Printers, Hurstpierpoint, W. Sussex.
Printed and bound in Great Britain by Cox & Wyman Ltd, Reading
Cartoons by Alan Ralph
©Rosemary Burr
ISBN - 0-948032-75-8

CONTENTS

Chapter Eight: Growing Pains

On the move. Price of growth. Franchise route. Reducing
unit cost. Spurt for growth. Adjusting your sights. Customers
control your destiny. Higher risk strategy.

Chapter Nine: White Heat of Technology

Technological buzz. Uncompromising course. Technological
imperative. Boosting profit margins. Snowball effect.
Marketing conundrum. Specialist manufacturing.

Chapter Ten: Twenty-Five Hour Day

Self-discipline. Secretarial buffer. Rigorous timetable.
Juggling act. Three helpmates. Cultural and rural
pursuits.

Chapter Eleven: Feminine Wiles

Twentieth century watershed. Survival instinct. Women's
touch. Dissolving the barriers. Good housekeeping approach.
Fields of competition. Risk takers. Unlocking your
potential.

Chapter Twelve: How to Win the Glittering Prizes

Setting your goal. Dash of realism. Inner Conviction.
Be prepared for the bumps. Get trained. Stick with it.
Build a team. Cultivate your bank manager. Know your
market. Develop your talents.

SECTION TWO

HOW THEY MADE IT TO THE TOP

INTRODUCTION: BOARDROOM LADIES

This is the story of twelve tough ladies. Not tough in the macho sense portrayed daily on our screens. They are not butch. Indeed, as a group they would probably score above average points for attractiveness, feminine charm and dress sense. Nor do they fall into the newly created category of Superwomen so vividly defined by Shirley Conran. They do not wield an iron with equal ease as a calculator. Some of them would no more dream of doing the housekeeping than lifting the bonnet of a car and tinkering with its contents.

New breed

These women are a new breed of ladies. They are in charge of their working lives. They don't kow tow to a male boss. The women described in this book run their own businesses with varying degrees of flair, imagination and acumen, but they all have one thing in common, a burning desire to succeed. For some this passion for excellence appears to have been instilled while they were still gurgling babies crawling around in nappies, for others circumstances, often tragic, have forced them into the position of either seizing the initiative or sinking into a mire of debt.

Despite the high proportion of women working, it remains a rarity to discover a female director at one of Britain's top companies. Industry, be it the shop floor, boardroom or union organisation is still dominated by men. To succeed in industry women have to be better than men and, again and again, prove themselves equal to the task.

In business the only proof required is black ink. Profits, earnings and growth. Perhaps one of the most revealing quotes made by a successful entrepreneur whose rags to riches story had captured the imagination was: "I had to succeed. I'm unemployable. If I didn't work for myself then I wouldn't work at all".

WHO'S WHO

● **Britt Allcroft**
Aged forty-three, married with two children.
Founded Britt Allcroft Ltd in 1981. She is managing director of the company which runs the Thomas The Tank franchise. Turnover rose above £1m in the year to June 30, 1986 and the company employs six staff.

● **Judith Davenport**
Aged forty-six, widowed with one child.
Finance director and co-founder of Channel Foods Ltd, the Truro based company which specialises in smoking fish caught in the local Cornish waters. Set up in 1980 the company now employs one hundred people and has a turnover of around £3.5m.

● **Elizabeth Gage**
Aged forty-nine, divorced, no children.
Managing director of Elizabeth Gage, she designs and sells her own jewellery. The company employs eleven staff on her premises, fifteen craftsmen and has a turnover of nearly £1m. It was set up in 1978.

● **Patricia Grant**
Aged forty-two, married with no children.
Managing director and co-founder of Norfrost, the freezer manufacturers. The company now employs one hundred and twenty staff and has a turnover of £5.9m.

● **Prudence Leith**
Aged forty-six, married with two children.
Managing director of Leith Group of Companies, which she founded in 1961. The group includes a restaurant, cookery school and farm. Turnover is around £2m and she employs a staff of one hundred.

● **Jennifer Loss**
Aged forty-six, married with four children.
Managing director of Charles Jourdan UK, vice president of Charles Jourdan International and fashion co-ordinator for

Charles Jourdan's women's products. The group's UK turnover is now around £8m and the company employs fifty staff in this country.

● Anita Roddick

Aged forty-four years. Married with two children.
Managing director and founder of The Body Shop, manufacturers and franchise retailers of natural based skin and hair products. Body Shop is now valued on the stock market at around £40m. There are now seventy-three branches in the UK and one hundred and four stores in sixteen countries around the world.

● Jenifer Rosenberg

Aged forty-four. Divorced, widowed and re-married. No children.
Founder and managing director of J&J Fashions, a private company which manufacturers women's clothes and supplies major high street retailers such as Marks & Spencer. Set up in 1974 the company now has a turnover approaching £25m and a staff of seven hundred and seventy-six.

● Anne Sargent

Aged sixty. Divorced and remarried. Three children. Two grandchildren.
Managing director of J&J Cash, a private company based in Coventry which manufacturers woven tapes, with a turnover of £2.7m. The company employs one hundred and twenty people.

● Jean Tyrell

Aged sixty-eight years. Three children. Two grandchildren.
Chairman of Sirdar, the publicly quoted textile company. She was managing director of the company between 1959 and 1979 and masterminded its growth and launch on the stock market. It is now valued at around £86m and employs over one thous and people.

● Jean Wadlow

Aged forty-three, divorced. No children.
Managing director and co-founder of Wadlow Grosvenor Inter-

national, the film production company. This is a private company set up in 1978. Current turnover is around £2m and more than twenty staff are employed.

● **Eileen Wiggins**
Aged fifty. Married. Two children.
Chairman and chief architect of Plastico, a private company which produces polystyrene cutlery. Turnover is approaching £5m and the company employs one hundred and twenty people.

True Grit

Together the experiences of these twelve women span forty years from the tail end of the second world war up to the middle eighties. Most of these ladies were born during the dark depressing days of World War Two, a time when many women were given the first chance to "man" the production lines which kept Britain's war machine from grinding to a halt. Their mothers may have been among the ladies who ran Britain while the men of that generation were overseas fighting for their king and country, but today these women are running businesses in their own right and proving that true British grit is equally common in both sexes.

CHAPTER ONE:
DUTIFUL DAUGHTERS

"I always knew I was special. I always wanted to be a star". Just the sort of remarks you would expect to hear from a television or film actress. In fact, these words came from Anita Roddick, the forty-four year old founder and mastermind behind The Body Shop. The lady who created an empire of over one hundred and seventy shops dispensing natural health products and cosmetics around the globe never had any doubts about her ultimate goal. She was determined to leave her mark, one way or another.

Anita Roddick is undoubtedly a success in the business world. It did not happen overnight. She cut her teeth on two less profitable ventures first, a hotel and a restaurant, before, in her own words, "thinking there must be an easier way of earning a living than this". Well, she found her yellow brick road down a Brighton lane in a damp shop in 1976, where she opened the first Body Shop selling just fifteen naturally made beauty products.

Today her company is worth more than £40m. Floated on the Stock Exchange in 1984, it quickly became the black umbrella brigade's darling and was the top performing share on the junior Unlisted Securities Market for that year. The flotation turned her into a paper millionairess and made her a household name.

She traces her success back to her family, her ethnic roots and the spirit of enterprise she supped along with the substantial Italian dishes at her parents' restaurant. Her parents were self-employed and her mother worked full time. Business matters were frequently discussed at home. Rolling up your sleeves and getting stuck in was a lesson she learnt early.

Trade Roots

"Making good" in Britain today all too often means going to the right school, wearing the right tie and becoming a member of the majical old boy network which is the key to future prosperity and social acceptance by your peers. For women such routes to success have not been available. Traditionally the main avenue to social status, wealth, position and even power was achieved through marriage.

Business is no respecter of persons, or sex. The market place is a rough, tough world with no easy rides going begging. The bottom line is profits, not gender. Many of today's successful women were brought up by families steeped in the tradition of trade. Judith Davenport, now Lady Wilcox, finance director and co-founder of Channel Foods, the second largest private employer in Cornwall, and a businesswoman of more than twenty years' standing, vividly describes the atmosphere in which she was brought up. "There wasn't that feeling of deep security which comes from a professional background. There was a feeling of money exchanging hands every day. My father used to say there are two sorts of people in this country. There are the aristocracy and landowning gentry, maybe 5%, who own just about everything and influence just about everything. Beyond that everybody is in the marketplace earning a living no matter what they may call themselves, no matter what fancy title they have. We are all in the marketplace trying for a living and you're as valid as anyone else to go in there and do it".

Judith Davenport comes from a background not just of traders but three generations of working women. Her mother worked along side her father in the family's high street shops scattered across the county of Devon. Her great grandmother operated the biggest fishing fleet in the West Country. It was the combination of what she describes as the "implicit background fishing knowledge" and her training in small business, later supplemented by a two year spell at the giant Ross Foods, which formed the ingredients in her now successful fish smoking business.

Family businesses clearly breed family businessmen and businesswomen. There is a spirit of adventure, of being in control over your own destiny which is lacking in so many areas of our lives today, not the least at work. Sara, a thirty-two year old Oxford graduate currently earning a substantial salary in the City has pangs to return to running a small business. She misses "the sense of involvement, of knowing every stage of the business. and seeing things through to a conclusion. The buzz just isn't there any more, even though the money is much better" she says.

Work Ethic
The twin themes of family business and the immigrant work

13

ethic crop up again and again. Jenifer Rosenberg is one of the few women running a successful clothing manufacturing company in this country. Her interest in business matters dates back to her childhood. "My parents had a small shop and I used to be much more fascinated in what they were selling and what was happening there than what was going on in school." School per se always played second fiddle for Jenifer. "I was never very academic — I was always smart enough to do enough work to keep me out of trouble but never enough to make me one of the stars. My headmistress summed it up by sending a report to my parents saying, "if Jenifer put as much effort and energy into her studies as she does into organising the school bazaar she would be a brilliant student."

Again Jenifer could turn to her mother as a role model. "My mother had a background of fashion and had always worked for a small company in the West End making clothes and had always been in fashion. So I'd heard about it and found it very fascinating". Jenifer did not immediately see herself as running a business but early on she knew "I did want an interesting and exciting career. So it was a combination of my commercial awareness and interest in fashion which counted when it came to a career decision time."

Jenifer, with her parents' help, singled out Marks and Spencer. "I looked around and felt it was one of the few companies which at that time, going back to the late '50's, gave women a career opportunity. They had a lot of very, very successful women in the company."

With no formal qualifications Jenifer opted to start in the post room. Her vowed intention was "quickly" rising to a buyer. When she first applied she was told "it's very difficult to become a buyer. It's no good to do it if you only want the glamour." She was not distracted easily from her goal. "I thought somebody's got to do it and it might as well be me." Fourteen years later at the age of thirty Jenifer quit M & S. "It took me three years to get into the buying department as a trainee. I was one of their senior buyers by the time I left with a buying power of £70m". Today Jenifer is the managing director of J & J Fashions, which manufacture a wide range of women's clothes and has a turnover approaching £25m.

14

Father's footsteps

"I always had in mind to help my father in business, it being a family business. There were no sons, just two daughters". For Jean Tyrell the outbreak of war catapulted her into the family textile business, Sirdar, based in Wakefield, but she never had any doubts this was to be her final destination. Jean was the oldest child and had just returned from a language course at Geneva when war broke out. "In September 1939 the men in the key positions had been called up and so I came in at that time to see what I could do to help". She found the remaining staff battling valiantly to cope with the unfulfilled orders.

Walking into a busy company bursting at the seams with work, she quickly discovered a niche for herself. "I looked around to see what was most in need of doing and I found a room full of letters from the general public. 'What are these doing here?' I asked and they said 'we've lost all the men who used to look after those', so I did it." Although her mother did not work full time Jean soon roped her into helping as well as the girl from the textile mill. "I worked all day and every night until about ten o'clock. I couldn't type so a lot of it was by hand but eventually I got a girl out of the mill and she did some and my mother helped me. When I got that done I looked around and said 'now what else can I do?" From chief letter writer she rose to managing director of one of the country's few textile companies to have survived and prospered the early 1980's recession. She is now chairman of the most profitable spinner in Britain.

Paternal model

Perhaps the clearest statement which underlines the importance of being brought up in a family business is made by Eileen Wiggins, now managing director of Plastico, manufacturers of plastic goods. While most women say they did not consciously model themselves on a particular named individual, Eileen, who inherited her father's business, said she modelled herself on her father and grandfather. Before the war her father had been employed by J. Lyons and then started a confectionery business.

Eileen went to Pitmans College and qualified in short hand, typing, accounting and business administration. She married at nineteen and her father gave the couple jobs running what was then a small, unimportant sideline to the main confectionery business, including the manufacture of "the humble cocktail stick". What started as a sideline developed under Eileen's care to become the mainstay of the business, whose name was changed to Plastico in 1972 to reflect this. Eileen puts down part of her success to the early stress "on working hard" and the importance of "good housekeeping". An only child she took complete control of the business in 1967 when her father became ill.

Breaking the mould

The routes to business success are many and varied. For some individuals it is the desire to excel per se which seems eventually to have led to the conclusion that they can only achieve what they wish by running their own show. Jean Wadlow's mother never worked, her father was not self-employed, but very early on she was attracted to the idea of being "in charge".

"The thing I remember when I was little was that my mother told me I had to be a school teacher and I was always taking class, so I think I probably learned leadership at an early age". She developed a passion for films early in life and after seven years as a secretary, decided that she wanted more than just a series of jobs.

She launched her career in advertising from the post of secretary to the chairman of one of the country's leading advertising agencies, Charles Barker. While still in her twenties she took over the group's film production company and seven years later she and Kyrle Simond arranged a management buy-out. Charles Barker Films became Wadlow Grosvenor International. Turnover in 1986 topped £2m, the company employs twenty-six people and has more than eighty corporate clients.

Secretarial stepping stone

From secretary to boss sounds as if it has the makings of a fairy story, but Jennifer Loss, the down-to-earth managing director of Charles Jourdan's UK operations, admits her path to the top has been hard and rocky. The daughter of band leader, Jo Loss, Jennifer says "I always knew I wanted to be different. I knew that I didn't want to be classified as the product of my father's success, although he has been an example all through my life. I always worked very hard, but I'm sure I didn't think of a career structure for life.''

Jennifer came from a background where work and struggle were natural and her parents were prepared to sacrifice their current comforts for a better future. "I came from an East End Jewish background where everybody works so hard to provide more for their children." However, Jennifer admits she was unusual in insisting on continuing to work after the birth of her first child.

"I got the job of bilingual secretary at Jordan at the age of nineteen. At twenty-one I took over public relations, at twenty-two I got married, at twenty-five had my first baby and became wholesale manager, which was unusual because most of my friends didn't work when they had children — they do now but at that time it was unusual.''

Success didn't come instantly for either Jennifer or her husband, a design engineer. "We didn't expect so much when we got married. I think it's important that we weren't allowed to go flying into instant success anywhere because we both had a very good training — that generation did. They all worked hard. We didn't have much money but we were always able to have fun.''

Throughout her life Jennifer "has done her own thing." With what she describes as "excellent support" from her husband in helping to run her home. She has four children, has boosted Jourdan's UK turnover from £350,000 in 1970 to £8m in 1985/6 and still finds time to squeeze in community work.

Success syndrome

Britt Allcroft was brought up by her mother and maiden aunt. She describes herself as a shy withdrawn child partly as the result of a stormy early childhood. Yet today she has created a highly successful business empire virtually overnight. In three short years she has taken a children's book about a train and turned it into a merchandising operation with a turnover of over £1m.

"I don't want to fail. Don't want to live with myself as a failure" she says. In fact her career has been a series of successes and self-created challenges. She appeared on tele-

17

vision in her teens, moved to be a presenter and then television producer in her early twenties. Became a freelance producer, married and then set up in business.

"I'm never satisfied. There's always got to be another challenge. It's something to do with being a perfectionist. I always learn from experiences as I go. If I feel unhappy I can quickly block things" she says.

Windey path

Peoples lives rarely move in straight lines. It may sound easy in retrospect to say as Anita Roddick has that she always knew she was "special", but for some women, entrepreneurship has rather taken them by surprise.

Elizabeth Gage is an award winning and top selling jewellery designer. She manages to combine the talents needed to produce startling and original jewellery year after year with the down-to-earth administrative ability necessary to run a business and handle the international marketing of her products.

"If you had asked me at seventeen, would I be a jewellery designer, I would have said no. I wasn't trained for that. In my thinking I was going to get married and have children. Life didn't really turn out that way for me."

Elizabeth was too ill to go to school until the age of twelve. She was educated at home and "never scholastically brilliant" as her illness resulted in her falling behind with school work. Her childhood was marred by lengthy separations from her parents, the war and chronic tuberculosis.

For Elizabeth there was no instant flash to point her to the road she was later to follow. "You don't always know what you want to do. I discovered very late but it came out of necessity to do something myself as I didn't have a family. I think if I had had a family I would not have had this need. I don't feel I could have run a business and had a family."

Elizabeth's divorce put paid to any ideas of marriage and a family and so she started training as a designer in 1964 at the John Cass College. She operated as a freelance designer for eight years, working for Cartier in New York and Jones of London. It was not until 1978 that she branched into business in a sizeable way with a studio in Beauchamp Place, a few streets away from Harrods. Six years later she took the plunge into the big time with a shop in fashionable Albemarle Street, tucked between Piccadilly and Bond Street. Her turnover now amounts to £1m and she has a staff of eleven.

In contrast, Patricia Grant, satisfied her ambitions early in life. "I wanted to join the Air Force. I had that ambition since I was about ten or eleven. I thought about the Wrens for a while but I eventually chose the air force. I had a career in that, which I enjoyed. I learnt a trade and a skill. I think it gives you very good background and sound discipline as well."
sound discipline as well."

Patricia joined the air force at seventeen, fell in love with a Scottish engineering apprentice while on holiday, left the forces at twenty-one and married. Going into business with her husband just came naturally.

"He'd just finished his apprenticeship and he was looking to start his own business. He was an electronics engineer and used to repairing white goods. I went into business with him. I looked after the book keeping and invoicing and serving in the shop while he did the TV side of things." It was pretty much a hand to mouth existence. The pair survived by getting agencies for Philips Televisions and eventually turning it into an "extended" family business. Patricia's sister-in-law and brother-in-law joined as well.

Matter of inheritance

A male relative was crucial to Anne Sargent's entry into the business world. Anne was an only child of rather older parents. She went to a number of schools because her father was in the army and the family were always on the move. For six years during the second world war she went to school at Oxford. Finally she was "finished" at The House of Citizenship in Oxfordshire.

"At Finishing School I learnt how to address bishops, duchesses, I learnt public speaking, which was useful, how to run a committee, typing, shorthand and quite a lot of useful public affairs — we used to do Home Affairs, International Affairs and what were called Colonial Affairs. It was the sort of widely based information that we hadn't had at school, so that it was really probably one of the most important things in my education."

19

At that stage she had no burning ambitions. One of her first jobs was as office junior at the National Association of Girls Clubs and Mixed Clubs for £3 a week. "I couldn't live on £3 a week so I was subsidised by my family. I did some other jobs — nothing of very great interest and then got engaged to a man who was going to be a don at Oxford. I spent the next seventeen years of my life in Oxford."

Looking back she reckons "in a funny way secretarial training is a very useful thing because it teaches you the importance of being an organised person." Her business life started abruptly in 1959 when her uncle Sir Reginald Cash died and left her a substantial interest in the family firm. Her mother and Sir Reginald were very close but she had no idea until the will was published that she would be left shares in J & J Cash, which makes nametapes, ribbons and trade labels.

Did Sir Reginald spot the birth of entrepreneurial talent or was there a more mundane reason for the gift? "I suspect he left me this interest because he considered that as I was married to a don, I'd never be able to make any money, which was quite an interesting view — and true." Still, not every mother of two left a share of a family business in one town, who lived nearly fifty miles away, would be prepared to divide their time between five days at home and two at the factory learning the ropes. Clearly her finishing school, the House of Citizenship, had nurtured Anne's managerial talents and her unwillingness to be a sleeping partner meant she had to throw herself headlong into discovering what made J & J Cash tick.

CHAPTER TWO:
FAMILY TIES

'Of course, if it hadn't been for my father, I wouldn't exist'

"Men make statements of fact, women make suggestions, they are always looking for approval in their actions. If a woman makes bold assumptions — which very few of them do — that she is important and what she does is important, then everybody else will accept it". Thus speaks the experience of Judith Davenport, who believes that without an initial surge of confidence women will remain tied to their apron strings.

Bold assumptions

The twelve successful women portrayed here have all made not just one, but many bold assumptions throughout their entrepreneurial lives. They exhibit an almost mystical faith in their ability to succeed, to survive and flourish through the hassles, problems and financial difficulties in their paths. So where do they derive this source of strength and power, this iron Bismarkian will to see events through to a successful conclusion?

The most obvious place to start seems to be their families and home lives. For some of the women this confidence, this flame of inner strength was forged out of adversity. Britt Allcroft's father left when she was five, Elizabeth Gage spent many of her formative years separated from her family. These ladies learned to cope with the conflicts and problems of the adult world early on.

For many successful women the belief in themselves was nurtured by close and warm family ties. Judith Davenport explains: "I'm from a very confident, almost cocky business background. My mother also worked. When we left home in the morning, nobody was left at home, everybody went into the world, into the marketplace. At the end of the day, you came back, shut the fortress door and all discussed how you'd got on. You licked your wounds and got ready to go out again next day. There was a great feeling of 'US' against the world."

When Jennifer Loss, daughter of band leader Jo Loss, was considering which career to follow her parents intervention and her acceptance of their advice was critical. "I'd always grown up amongst music and I love the theatre. I wanted to go into theatre on the production side. Very early on, sort of eighteen or nineteen, my father put his foot down — and one accepted it in those days — you couldn't actually have a family and children and career at night, he said — and he was probably right."

Later on, at a crucial crossroads in her business career, it was to the two closest men in her life her father and husband that she turned to for advice and moral support. "My father is a professional man and he'd never have been successful for all those years without being a good businessman as well. He always pays attention to detail. Yes, I think he was probably most helpful together with my husband", says Jennifer Loss.

Similarly, when Jenifer Rosenberg describes the hunt for her first job she says "my parents and I looked around". After Anne Sargent inherited a stake in the family firm and decided that rather than being a passive investor, she would spend two days a week away from her Oxford home learning the business, it was her parents who put her up.

The women who went into family businesses appeared to have formed a very vital and strong link with their fathers, on whom they consciously or unconsciously moulded themselves. References to their fathers, what their fathers said and did, are scattered throughout their comments. By all accounts these relationships were not plain sailing, but based on mutual admiration. Not all the fathers spotted the depth of their daughter's talents but all seemed to take it for granted that their daughters would get stuck into the family business. Few would dream quite how successful their offspring would turn out in shaping, developing and channeling frequently small businesses into new and growing areas for the future.

Husband's role

It has become something of a cliche to assume successful women are either single or divorced. While this is indeed true of two of the women I spoke to, the majority have found their husbands a key factor in their success. Many work alongside their partner in the business, with the women tending to exhibit marketing skills, the ability to handle staff relations and outside suppliers with relative ease while the man handles the longer term planning and financial angles.

Jenifer Rosenberg has been married to three men. She divorced her first husband while still a high flying executive at M & S. Her second husband set up J&J Fashions for her and advised her in the early days. "My husband was obviously a great help. I needed his advice and equally I used to advise on the ranges he was putting together because when you are only trying to keep sixteen machinists going you don't need many ranges." Unfortunately, two years after the business was set up, Jennifer's husband died. "It was very traumatic and I was on my own."

Six years later she met her third husband, "I'd been on my own for six years but I remarried four years ago. My husband is in the business too now — Ian had a textile company when we met. We didn't meet through business, we met through friends and we found we had this tremendous common interest being in fashion and so we brought the two businesses together."

Working in tandem

For Patricia Grant her marriage and business have been inter-woven for the whole of her adult life. Her husband, the trained engineer is in charge of technical matters. They have clearly delineated areas of responsibility in the company. "I have my jobs, speaking to my customers, dealing with suppliers. I look after the office staff, check with the accountants regarding stock control. My husband is the engineer in the company. He designs machines to make machines in a lot of cases." Of course there are times then they have disagreements, but their overriding joint desire to see the business flourish usually helps iron out the problems. "I think when you are working close together or in the same field there will be conflicts but so long as it's not on a personal basis and you are both looking for what's good in the company. If we disagree about something it's because we both want what's best for the company, it's not because I disagree with him because he's my husband or on principle or vice versa. And, if after all he said "yes, darling, go ahead" all the time, it's not going to get us very far."

Role defining

So working together can in some circumstances strengthen a marriage, provided each partner has clearly defined areas of expertise, the women are confident enough to fight their corner and a strategy can be developed for handling and defusing the natural string of conflicts. Often it works best when women have been successful before their husbands joined them full time. For example, Britt Allcroft is full of praise for her husband's qualities "we complement each other; I do the selling, he does the administration." However, she did notice when they were introduced as husband and wife in a business context, that all the subsequent conversation was addressed solely to her husband. "I fiercely protect my position. I keep my own name. I started the business alone, my husband joined later."

One couple, the Davenports, found in the end that their business relationship has flourished even though their twenty-two year long marriage ended. In business, they are complementary. Her strengths are in planning, finance and strategy whereas her former husband's trump hand is marketing and selling. Her husband did not join the family business straight away, "he became a commercial traveller and a very good one. Eventually he came into the famiy business, by which time I had grown confident and my son had grown up."

Third generation

The Wiggins have also worked together throughout their married life and raised two children. The family thread has been wound one stage further with the recent arrival of their daughter in the business. They too complement each other. Eileen is outgoing, keen on new ideas and stresses the importance of design and marketing. Her husband is rather quieter, the thinker, urging caution where necessary and keeping a rein on the finances.

Women who are married to men in other fields seem to have the best chance of making a success of both their careers and marriage if their husbands are not surprisingly successful in their own right but also involved in creative work in some way. Prue Leith, for example, is married to author Rayne Kruger. She reckons "husbands do slow you down" and there are basically two feasible strategies to adopt; either marry young, have kids straight away and then start a business, or marry later once the business is established and the hurly-burly of those early crunch days are just a memory. She married in her mid-thirties and now says she leads virtually two separate lives.

Work is reserved for London and home matters are restricted to the country.

Picking "Mr Right"

Jennifer Loss explains "the first thing is that I'm old enough to remember when divorce was very much frowned upon. It was up to us to make the marriage work. Secondly I was very fortunate in having a husband who was creative, very quiet but very, very bright and he grew and expanded. I think it must be very difficult if you grow in different directions and I'm not sure you can always tell that. Thirdly, we worked hard at our marriage."

Jean Tyrell, now a grandmother, has by all accounts an exceptionally understanding husband. He turned down a prestigious job in a growing Canterbury practice to stay in Wakefield near his wife's work. "He found a job in this area to suit me. He had a job offered in Canterbury to go into a big practice with other doctors and we considered it, but he said you'd like to go on with your work, wouldn't you? and I said, yes, if it is possible — and so he found something as a consultant anesthetist. He's gone on finding jobs in Leeds, Wakefield and Pontefract so that I could go on. He's retired now".

Jean admits her husband's decision to base his career moves on her business needs was unusual. "It played an important part for me to be able to stay here. It isn't easy for a man and woman to continue in their own jobs unless they live near a town where the wife can find a job that fits and the husband can still carry on his job."

Not all women were so lucky in their choice of husband. Jean Wadlow sums it up, "I was married very young and grew out of it — it seems like another world." Marriage is now no longer on the agenda. "I think when you take on responsibilities you get involved — not just materially but psychologically — there is a price. You cannot afford to have the luxury of having a husband and being all cosy." For Jean her business is now a surrogate family, "my whole life is running this company — it is my family, my social life everything. I don't have any children — this is my baby, this company."

Balancing act

Although most successful women stress the juggling act of balancing demands of a husband, children and work, few rule out marriage so systematically. Indeed three of them, Jenifer Rosenberg, Judith Davenport and Anne Sargent, divorced and then remarried while running and expanding their respective businesses.

Combining marriage and work has become increasingly routine for women in Britain during the past three decades. Being boss does give you certain scope for flexibility, even if it places more demands on your time than a nine to five job. Here, the role of women's parents tends to reassert itself. Unfortunately, the idea of the extended family, or even the family unit itself, has faded from fashion, but for most of these women who successfully managed to combine entrepreneurial success with husband and children, it was their mothers and that rather old fashioned figure, the British Nanny, who often proved vital.

The "Nanny" factor

Judith Davenport had her son when she was twenty-three and just finding her feet in the business world. "I automatically had a nanny, in fact the same nanny which had looked after me. My parents saw no reason for me to stay at home — I wasn't ill and the precedent in the family was for women to go to work, so I never had any thoughts about not being at home with my son."

For Jean Tyrell a trio of helpers kept the family under constant supervision. "I engaged a very good nanny. When I had my first daughter, my mother lived nearby. My husband being a doctor didn't have to go out too far — apart from being on call at nights he wasn't away at nights — so when I went in those days to Australia, New Zealand, South Africa — and all over the place — he was at home, plus a Nanny who looked after the children, plus mum and they all sort of stretched themselves while I was away and really covered extremely well for me."

"I did have tremendous help from mother who lived just up the lane. She used to come and take the children out for walks and leave nanny to get on in the house and I had women as helps — I had a lot of those which enabled me to put in full time here." As well as this extra feminine array of willing hands and able bodies, Jean Tyrell admits the children were sent to boarding school rather earlier than they might have gone had she been a full time mother.

When Jennifer Loss had her first child she also opted for that standby, the British Nanny. "I took on a nanny. I think I was earning maybe fourteen pounds a week. I paid the nanny six or seven pounds." She has four children and agrees it is difficult to keep the balance between the various parts which go to make up her life. "It's quite difficult running a family and a career, keeping the balance and not forgetting your husband who tends to come last. You've got to be married to a very extra-ordinary kind of man for him to put up with that kind of structure. I was lucky because Robert always worked at home since the early seventies — or close to home — and has very much lent a hand in bringing up the children."

Women who work with their husbands and do not have children before they start running the business together tend to find it more difficult to start a family. For Jennifer Rosenberg the time never seemed right. "Having children was one of those things which just never happened. My first marriage was a disaster and my second we were only together for two years. Then I was on my own for six years and that was probably the time when one would have had a family. I have now been married four years. I have two grown-up step children I am very close to. I'm also very close to my sister and she's got three children."

Patricia Grant, who works alongside her husband at their freezer manufacturing company, also explains her decision not to have children in virtually the same words as Jenifer Rosenberg, "well, it just didn't happen — we weren't bothered — we've got two dogs."

Old fashioned values

Not surprisingly, there are no single mums along this band of successful female entrepreneurs. On the whole, although these women can be considered as daring insofar as they have broken the taboo of females in the boardroom, in their family and domestic lives they are remarkably conservative and tend to stress the old fashioned values. Jean Wadlow, perhaps, represents more typically the lifestyle we have become familiar with in the eighties. She is determinedly single and single minded with it. "I would say that anyone who really wants a career can't be preoccupied with looking for a husband or marriage. People say to me, you're going to regret this when you are old — you'll be lonely. But there's no insurance it would continue. Marriage can come to an end. I think the only insurance you can have is being comfortable in your own company."

Family fortress
The women with children stress the strength they derive from this and a close family. There is a sense of unity derived from jointly battling with the range of problems thrown up by the world outside, which at most times seems to compensate for the difficulties created within their domestic circle. This is summed up by Judith Davenport when she stressed "to have a large and supporting family is the biggest ingredient in success."

CHAPTER THREE:
YEARS OF APPRENTICESHIP

'Behind every successful woman is an envious man'

The stories of some of these women may read like fairy tales of instant success, recognition and wealth. In fact, most had to graft away for a decade or more before the first glimmer of really "big" money came their way. They had to learn about what made business tick, build up contacts, develop a flair for spotting a sound commercial possibility and the confidence to run their own show. "It all just came together at the right time with the right idea" is how several of the women explained their success.

The employee route

Not surprisingly, the ladies whose chose to learn their skills by working for other people tended to be in industries where women were accepted, had traditionally done rather well and where their path to the top, although difficult, was not impossible. As Jean Wadlow, now head of her own film production company explained, "I was a secretary in the stock exchange — and at that time there was no chance at all of getting on to the stock exchange because it just didn't happen for women. The careers open to women in stockbrokers' offices were very limited, so I decided I'd either have to go into law or advertising. I saw an advertisement for a position in an advertising agency for a secretary, I applied for it and got it."

The job as it turned out was working for the chairman of Charles Barker. Jean was given her first taste of film work, while still working for the chairman. "I became the head of television's personal assistant when I was still secretary to the chairman — the chairman started semi-retirement at that time. I found that I like commercials and films and that world and took to it extremely well. Then the poor chap died very suddenly and I asked if I could have the chance of doing the job and was given it."

This was the turning point in Jean's career. Still in her early twenties, she convinced the management to let her have a trial run at the job of supervising the television unit. Needless to say, Jean proved a big hit. "It was quite a lot to take on. I did it. I got the rewards and became quite a celebrity in the world of advertising."

Her initial success was the stepping stone for the next major breakthrough. "And then in 1971 the whole group split up into different companies and I was asked if I'd like to head up the film company in the group, which was then making documentary films. And we made a success of that. I really used the contacts I had made in my advertising experience. We got ourselves quite a good reputation and good clients."

When the chance of going solo presented itself, Jean was ready and more than able. In 1978 the then chairman of Charles Barker, Kyrle Simond, and Jean arranged what is now fashionable to call a management buy-out. They purchased the film company from Charles Barker and Wadlow Grosvenor Productions was created.

Learning on the job

Another lady who started life as a secretary and ended up as boss is Jennifer Loss. Written off by her schoolmistress at St Paul's girls school as "really not very bright" she was sent to the Lycee to learn French at the age of sixteen and also took a typing course. At nineteen she emerged into the world searching for a job as a bi-lingual secretary. The agency sent her for an interview with Charles Jourdan. Her then best friend, now sister-in-law, had gone to the Sorbonne in Paris and raved about Charles Jourdan, so Jennifer decided to accept the job.

"I got the job with Jourdan as a bilingual secretary at the age of nineteen. That was on 5th December 1959 and I've been here ever since," she explains. Jourdan's operations were relatively small at that stage with about a dozen employees working alongside Jennifer in the Bond Street shop.

"I was taught to keep books, do inventories, prepare shoes for the window — preparing a man's shoe by hand — it took about an hour and a half. The boss pulled it apart if it wasn't perfect. It was very much the business training of the old days, which doesn't exist now. If we were busy we were there to one in the morning — there was no overtime. I earned nine pounds ten shillings as my first wage."

Two years later Jennifer took over the public relations side of the business and the following year married. "I was travelling abroad to France to the factory at twenty-one or twenty-two, which, looking back, was actually exceptional experience and great fun." She was promoted to the post of wholesale manager, but even so says "I didn't think of myself as a high powered executive — I enjoyed my job."

As chance would have it, the crunch time for Jennifer came in 1971. "A series of circumstances arose where I actually had to defend my job against a situation with another man who worked in the company. It was the first time I had been confronted with this and with a lot of discussion with both my father and my husband I decided that it was worth defending this job." Women are traditionally taught to be peacemakers not protagonists, so it is hardly surprising that Jennifer took some time before consciously deciding it was worth entering the fray. "I wasn't brought up as an extremely tough lady but very professional in terms of background. A showdown took place over a year or so. I ended up finding myself in a position which actually I hadn't sought as general manager."

Corporate launch pads

An increasing number of people are starting their business, because after a period of relatively rapid success within a corporation, they look around and discover the next big leap is going to take another decade. By this time they have learnt the basics of their trade and, if they are ambitious, see no reason why they should wait around for their superiors to deign to recognise their achievements. Two women who made spectacular successes of their early careers and then turned their backs on these in search for enterprising pastures new are Jenifer Rosenberg and Britt Allcroft.

Jenifer Rosenberg knew what she wanted that first day she joined Marks & Spencer as a teenager in the post room. It was to be a buyer. By the time she was thirty she was a senior buyer with a failed marriage as the price of her success. "In the early seventies everything started opening up at Marks & Spencer and they were planning to open stores in Europe and I was on the European committee. They started importing a lot of fabric from America, so I was always in America and that created a disastrous marriage."

The job which had effectively killed off her first marriage was however responsible for Jenifer's first meeting with her second husband. "While I was at Marks & Spencer I met my second husband — a supplier — and managing director of

Selincourt. Selincourt at that time were very large suppliers to M&S." At this stage Jenifer could not see how to develop her career further at M&S. "I was a buyer and really at one of the most senior positions I could possibly get to and I really didn't know where my career was going from there. Something inside me said 'you've got to start something new'. Being ambitious, when my husband, who unhappy about me working there, put the proposition that he would start for me a small manufacturing company, that seemed the answer. It was all done in conjunction with M&S and they were very happy because if I was going to supply them they were going to get the best of both worlds — they had someone who knew the M&S market and customers, and equally would eventually understand the manufacturing side." So Jenifer puts that crucial decision to set up in business down to "circumstances".

For Britt Allcroft, the lady who has made a business out of merchandising Thomas The Tank, circumstances had little to do with her decision to quit the relative security of paid employment in the television industry and go it alone. She was always looking for new challenges. While still at school she had tried her hand at interviewing local celebrities on the issues of the day and in the swinging sixties when the face of youth was in its ascendancy she presented current affairs programmes for Southern Television. She quickly tired of the presenter role and switched her attention to writing and production, spending spells at the BBC and Southern.

After ten years in television Britt took the plunge and went freelance. Between 1973 and 1979 she began to build the entrepreneurial skills which were to prove so vital later on. She developed her connections in television and the world of entertainment. Among her first projects were a series of meetings between the public and celebrity DIY experts as well as arranging gala charity nights.

Her big break was very much of her own making. It took considerable courage and the confidence to mortgage their home. She was researching for a television programme and met Reverend Awdry, author of a series of books on Thomas The Tank. She decided not only to make a television programme out of the books but that the series had the potential to support a merchandising operation. She bought both the world rights to the books and all merchandising rights. Britt Allcroft Ltd had started down the track which was to lead to the company's turnover to over £1m in just five years and dramatic growth.

Keeping it in the family

While those women who opted for full time employment initially spent their early working lives learning the basic skills of production, marketing and managing small groups of people, those who joined small friendly businesses straight away tend to have developed rather different talents early on. Running a small business is hectic, fun, demanding and full of risks. From day one you need to learn how to cope with cash flow hiccoughs, mixed success and failure, planning your overall strategy and financing expansion as and when it comes.

In an age of business degrees and highly paid consultants it is popular to knock the "school of life" brigade as unfashionable, neolithic and out of touch with the modern world. However, many of today's successful entrepreneurs lack formal business education. What they do have, however, is the ability to recognise their own qualities and shortcomings. If needed they have brought into the company people with the necessary qualifications.

Two outstanding ladies who learnt their skills in one set of family businesses and then built upon them to develop new, fresh and thriving enterprises are Anita Roddick and Judith Davenport. Anita Roddick's meteoric rise to success has become something of a media truism, trotted out at every occasion. The seeds of Anita's fortune were sewn over at least a decade. Her teacher's training, her two previous business ventures alongside husband Gordon in both the hotel and restaurant business plus her travels around the world where she picked up hints on natural beauty products. All these strands of life came together in 1976. Her timing was perfect. She thought she had produced a range of products appealing to the fringe student "brown rice brigade" instead she found a much wider customer profile.

Traditional pattern

Equally a long time in the germinating was the eventual shape of Judith Davenport's current thriving fish smoking business,

Channel Foods. "I left school at seventeen and then went to technical college and did a business studies course. I didn't do the secretarial course as such, which would have been much more correct." Her parents owned a string of about twenty small shops, "my father thought if I was good at bookwork — that would be the thing — there were lots of little spots I could fill."

For Judith Davenport going into the family business was a matter of course, "that was what I was trained to do and I joined the family business as simple as that. Nothing adventurous." In fact, her early life pretty much matched the pattern laid out for her by the family. She married, had a child, inherited the nanny who had brought her up and who subsequently cared for her son, and continued to work.

Her husband was a commercial traveller and later joined the business providing a useful injection of marketing expertise into the company. The family firm was much as it had always been but a small wholesale company had been established to supply the chain of stores. Life looked set to continue on its well trodden route when two disparate events on either side of the Channel pushed Judith Davenport into a completely new area of business.

The first event sounds somewhat routine nowadays. A holiday in France, the sun shining by the quayside and Judith Davenport with her first husband, Keith, eating langoustine. "'Why can't we buy these in England?' asked Keith. 'I don't know' I replied. So the next morning we bought some on the quay. I went and bought them because I could speak French — I'd worked there for a while. Keith being very good at marketing said 'OK if we buy more than we need maybe I can sell them to somebody — that way we can bring some over for ourselves.' The next day he sold some to Harrods and Fortnums."

The second event was the death of Judith Davenport's grandmother. "The langoustine had been a novelty — not something we had taken very seriously. Then my grandmother left me a trawler fishing for scallops and losing money outrageously. I needed to do something with these boats, these scallops." So they decided to start a two-way service, shipping scallops to the Continent and bringing langoustine back here.

They soon discovered it was much cheaper to set up a small processing unit to strip the scallops from their shells and then pack them more effectively into the cross channel boats. In retrospect it sounds simple, but it wasn't all plain sailing. "It isn't all that easy. There's the horrendous moments when the whole consignment you took to France gets rejected because you sold them spider crabs and they're all dead."

Judith Davenport and her first husband, with whom she still runs their newest operation, were a complementary pair. "It was a good combination. Me as the financial planner, organiser, using the things I had learnt from running small shops — planning your time, planning your products, spreading your payments, and Keith with his sales and marketing flair."

Like father, like daughter

One of the most common ways of going into business on your own account, be it for a man or woman, is simply to take over the reins of a family firm and guide its expansion. Families with no sons to inherit have three options, to sell out, bring in outsiders in key roles or permit the female offspring to have a go.

Jean Tyrell is now chairman of the publicly quoted textile company Sirdar. Started in 1880 in Osset, near Wakefield the company specialised in the manufacture of hand knitting yarn, rug yarn and canvas. At the turn of the century Sirdar moved to its present site in Wakefield itself. In 1938 before the outbreak of World War Two is started publishing leaflets with knitting designs and developed some sales overseas. The Second World War left the company bereft of personnel and Jean, then twenty-one joined to help out her father. She started by sorting out the irate correspondence from customers who had dispatched their six old pence for a knitting leaflet and not been sent anything back. After tidying up that little problem, she turned her mind to developing new business, concentrating on developing relations with the press.

"I was in a little office and I had on my right hand side our chief designer, who was really managing the production of the leaflet section, and there was my father and his main manager — everybody else had literally almost gone, except for the odd

37

was a question of making what you could and I was very promotion minded at the time. I saw if I could get editorials in magazines this was fabulous. I went and said that I would have six advertisements throughout the year and when I have those six advertisements, I want solo editorials for Sirdar — and they said yes — and it happened. You couldn't do it like that today.''

For the next few years Jean concentrated on developing her contacts in the magazine world, generating good editorial for Sirdar and even developing special patterns for individual magazines which could then be knitted in Sirdar wool. ''We got a tremendous lot of publicity by going a talking to the editors — I knew them all in those days. They were almost martinets in their field. They came in the morning, went to have their hair done, then swanned in at ten thirty in the morning — and were real queen bees. It was quite another world.''

While Jean was developing the company's advertising and promotional campaign, the production decisions were still being taken back in Wakefield. ''I went along with all that was being produced. We had a sales manager who looked after the representatives and he would report back what he felt was needed out in the field. Of course we didn't do fancy yarns at that stage. It was all just very much bread and butter dull knittings.''

It was not until Sirdar went public in 1952 that Jean went on the board and became more actively involved in the sales side. Seven years later Jean and her father learnt that the then managing director had cancer. ''I had to be prepared to be even more involved which I hadn't imagined I was going to do. I was made joint managing director, so that when he died two years later, I was left as managing director. My father died about five months later, so I was left literally holding the baby.''

Death acts as catalyst

Eileen Wiggins was also thrust into the hot seat by the death of her father. An only child she joined the family business running what was then regarded as a secondary division specialising plastics. The main moneyspinner was confectionery. In lad who was still not called up. It was all very primitive and it 1967 her father had a stroke and she was made a director. Eileen had to juggle with the triple stress of running the business, helping her mother cope with her father's illness and manage her own domestic affairs.

Two deaths feature in the story of Anne Sargent's entry into the world of business. After she had inherited shares in the family business from her uncle and decided to learn what made J&J Cash tick, she was made a director. "As soon as I got there I discovered that the very last thing anybody wanted to teach me was how it worked and I was just passed around from department to department. They made me a director but of course I didn't do anything and I couldn't quite understand how things worked. It all seemed very strange. It was an old fashioned business run very much on paternal lines."

The company specialised in what was broadly called narrow fabrics. Founded in 1846 to make silk ribbons, J&J Cash had diversified into jacquard ribbons, woven name tapes and printed labels. By the 1930's it was one of the bigger employers in Coventry with staff of around one thousand.

The first thing which struck Anne was the lack of clear lines of communication. "The foreman would go to the directors and say 'we think we should do this, but the managers have told us to do that, what should we do?' It was incredible when you think about it." She did her best to learn as much as possible about the company, its production techniques and staff management. "I went round and learnt a certain amount, I learnt how ribbons were made, how a jacquard machine worked, all the various things. It was in a site of four and a half acres. Some of the buildings had been there since 1956."

Six years after first setting foot inside J&J Cash's Coventry plant Anne emerged as chairman. "And then in 1965 we had quite a dramatic happening — the man who was chairman, who was connected by marriage to the family, suddenly dropped dead. So there was a crisis. The man who was a cousin, a descendant of the Cash's, was joint managing director, so he said 'shall I be chairman and managing director'. I said I don't think that's a good idea. You be managing director and I'll be chairman." In retrospect, Anne says she doesn't reckon she was very good at the job of being chairman but "that was when I really started to have some influence in the firm."

Dramatic currents

If the routes some of these women were pushed along to the top seem rather bizarre or dramatic, perhaps that simply reflects the fact women are not regarded as natural successors for the post of managing director. One of the traditional arguments used to support the theory that women don't have the makings of entrepreneurs is that unlike men they don't like taking risks. In fact, women have always taken risks.

Their social status and often wealth has been bound up through the ages with their husbands. They have had only one card to play, their feminity, and before the era of easy divorce only one hand with which to capitalise on their assets.

All of the women portrayed in this book have taken risks, thrived on doing so and become addicted to the thrills and spills of the commercial world. Some actively sought the role of entrepreneur for themselves as the most acceptable way of earning a living, others became victims of circumstances and in mastering the often tragic events in their lives learned they too could cope with taking risks.

What they all have in common is an incredible belief in themselves. Again and again, when faced with huge daunting challenges which if analysed in the cold light of day would seem virtually insurmountable, they simply buckled down to the task at hand — and flourished on whatever was flung at them.

CHAPTER FOUR:
EARLY DAYS

'Whenever a woman enters his office to ask for a loan he always stands up before refusing'

Most small business proprietors given the opportunity will reel off a list of injustices or supposed slights they received when they were starting out. Typical bugbears range from bank managers "who don't understand them" through to landlords demanding rent up front. Whether women expect to face these type of problems and therefore moan less, I don't know, but what grouses there were seemed relatively tame compared to the catalogue of woes many of their male colleagues enumerate.

Often the first hurdle for the would-be enterprising lady is getting together the wherewithall to make her assault on the business world. Anita Roddick quickly learnt the importance of "playing by the rules" when, kids in tow, she failed to convince a bemused bank manager about the merits of lending her money to start the first Body Shop. She returned a second time, accompanied by her husband and presented a detailed business proposal with a suitable number of projections and statistics. The pair emerged triumphant.

The money trap

Many of the ladies interviewed reckoned that raising finance was one of the major areas where women face greater difficulties than men. This view was shared by Anita Roddick, Elizabeth Gage, Prudence Leith, Jennifer Loss, Jenifer Rosenberg and Anne Sargent. Obviously their response partly reflects their own experience, the women who did not think their sex was a handicap in the finance stakes were largely those who sought cash to expand a mature existing business rather than a greenfield development.

Jenifer Rosenberg had to cope with the sharp end of the bank manager's tongue in the height of the property crisis in 1974. That was the year, with her husband's full support, she quit her job at M&S to start a small manufacturing company in the North East of England. "It was horrendous. We actually signed the lease on the factory and with our collateral we got a certain amount of overdraft at the bank." Then came the collapse of property prices, the secondary banking crisis and the crash in share prices. "The collateral just faded into oblivion and our overdraft was cut in half — just like that, just one phone call. We were committed, we'd signed a lease on the building for twenty-five years. I had personal guarantees everywhere. The house we had was mortgaged and if we failed we'd be turned out on the street."

What follows will probably ring true to most people who have started small businesses and juggled with cheques to keep their creditors quiet. "We were only operating three days a week on a shoestring, because the overdraft had been cut in half. I can remember on a Thursday when the M&S cheque used to arrive, I used to wait for it to come so I could take it to the bank — it had to go in for Friday to pay the wages. I even used to think twice about making a phone call," explained Jenifer Rosenberg.

On the whole bank managers are by nature, training and selection a cautious bunch of people. It is their job first and foremost to guard the depositors' money not create new jobs and businesses. They naturally tend to distrust budding entrepreneurs with no experience, short of a business plan who march into their offices asking for huge cash hand outs. Interestingly enough, just as in the investment world, women in business tend to be relatively cautious about borrowing money. Part of this is wrapped in the desire to keep their hard won independence and part is simply that no one ever showed them how the big wheels of finance operate.

Self-financed

Jenifer Rosenberg learned her lesson from that very first phone call when her bank manager slashed the company's overdraft. "I've always known from day one that unless you are making a profit you can't inject back all the money and you can't milk a business. The business has been mainly self-financed. We've had very few borrowings from the bank. I felt it was important to keep the money in the business, particularly our type of business which is very capital orientated." She later financed a massive £2m new computerised cutting centre largely out of profit.

Elizabeth Gage, whose turnover is worth around one million pounds, says "I started the business on being given either one thousand pounds or one thousand dollars — I don't remember which it was, it was so long ago — to buy some raw materials. That's what everything you see today is out of — that amount of money. I haven't put any money into the business at all, nor

43

have I had to borrow any — I've made it work, because I feel if it can't work on the small scale it's not going to work with lots of money coming."

Beating the bank manager's block

Women joining existing businesses with a long history in the locality and existing bank relationships, don't find they run into the same type of bank manager's block. Jean Tyrell is full of praise for her former local bank manager who allowed them to borrow a sum equivalent to one year's profit. "We were backed by Barclays, which was rather splendid at the time. We had a very good local bank manager who obviously believed in us. He was a far seeing man — different from the ordinary type of manager that one would get in Wakefield. He's gone now."

Belief in the borrower's ability to repay the loan is the be-all and end-all for bank managers. Ultimately it's simply a matter of blind faith based on past judgement and assessment of both the borrower's business capabilities and the strength of the product or service they are hoping to sell.

Once women learn the art of putting together professional proposals and arguing their case in the correct manner, provided they have a bank manager with an entrepreneurial streak, the evidence suggests they can turn on the cash tap. Judith Davenport set up her second business afresh in 1980 after a spell working with Ross Foods, who had taken over her previous venture. Her years with Ross were "a very good thing. They taught me how large companies operate. I learnt a very different way of approach, of raising finance."

In 1980, when she decided to set up a company to smoke fish caught locally in Cornwall, she built on the experience culled at Ross Foods. "I decided to run a highly geared company. Money was fairly easily available at that time." She went to the bank armed with data supporting her case, forward projections and a good team of professionals. She was very fortunate with her bank manager, who she said was unusual for someone whose main business was dealing with personal customers, as he was prepared to back a speculative venture. "If you keep the bank informed they will help you all they can." She found the need to keep the bank in touch and account for each penny, a sound discipline. "It kept us very much on our toes."

44

Getting the business

If persuading the mostly male establishment to part with funds is more difficult for women, most reckon they have the edge when it comes to gaining new business. Put simply, they unanimously believe that men would prefer to deal with a woman rather than another man — given the choice.

Britt Allcroft, who has persuaded over one hundred companies to pay for the right to produce Thomas the Tank merchandise thinks several of her first interviews were granted partly because she was a woman. She reckons some of the men she contacted were intrigued and prepared at least to let her get a foot in the door. A privilege they would not have extended to a man in the same position.

Jean Wadlow, who numbers more than a third of the top one hundred companies in the country among her clients, reckons most high powered male executives have a soft spot for a well turned out lady. "A lot of people would rather deal with an attractive woman than a man." The secret she argues is "to enjoy being a woman and let the men go on being masculine."

Natural negotiations

Skillful negotiation is critical at all times in running a business but especially at the start when cash is usually short and it's important to build up a list of satisfied customers relatively quickly. Patricia Grant, managing director of Norfrost Freezers thinks women are natural negotiators.

"If you look at most women in business — or in the house — they are negotiating all the time. At home, for example, with the kids it's eat up your tea or you won't get your pocket money or whatever." Patricia revels in both buying for her company and arranging the price at which the goods are dispatched. "I like the negotiating side — getting people into tight corners on prices. I know what it's like when they try it with me — my customers — and you've got to try and wangle yourself out of it."

She reckons women tend to be better buyers than men "A housewife can teach you more about economics than you'd learn at university. Men never look at prices when they are shopping. If you say to a man, how much did that cost, he'll say I don't know — I just grabbed the first thing that looked like a packet of cakes."

To most Englishwomen, the French are a romantic nation, so it's rather surprising to hear from Jennifer Loss that senior executives at Charles Jourdan frequently ignore the fact she is a woman altogether. "The shoe manufacture and design business is a masculine world — there are women buyers but in the production it's very masculine. Working in France has been an unusual experience — I've been called "monsieur" and treated like a man more often than not," she says.

The art of persuasion

Business deals are often completed amidst an almost deafening thud of egos sparring, clashing and ultimately turning into conqueror and conquered. Women traditionally are pacifiers, they don't tend to initiate clashes, to launch attacks in the same way as men are taught to do. In business, this can be both an advantage in the early days and a shortcoming later on when expansion by takeover is often the most effective route.

This desire to please, to assume that you as a woman are in the wrong rather than the man, has led women to develop skills of persuasion. They learn to play on people's weak spots, often their vanity, and to cajole, wheedle or negotiate to obtain their ends. These skills are very useful in obtaining business, as is the traditional approach adopted by women of leaving their men thinking they have won. "Keeping your customer satisfied" and "the customer is always right" are two slogans which are second nature to many women.

On the negative side, women have to learn to be ruthless. "I had to learn that not everybody was going to like you. I had to fire someone who was bringing their personal problems to the office, even though I had a great deal of sympathy with the problems she was facing," said one woman. Another added, "I used to think about having to fire someone with dread and be more worried about it than now. Now I think it's not just for me, I'm getting rid of this person, but for the whole team. One bad influence spoils the whole atmosphere."

Motivating factor

The art of persuasion counts not just when dealing with suppliers, customers or outside interests, but also within the business's own four walls. Small businesses in particular tend to be run by charisma rather than bureaucracy. This is style of management which women usually find easier to handle and perpetuate.

For example, Elizabeth Gage says, "I have a very good and loyal team now without whom I couldn't do this if I didn't have their support — it's a joint effort — we work very much together and if we do well, they do well."

Similarly, when Jenifer Rosenberg started in those grim days of scrimping, saving and even pausing before she lifted the telephone up and spent precious money, she managed to hold her staff together. "I have a wonderful team of people — I don't think anybody does anything on their own, and they've been very loyal. When my husband died they needn't have stayed with me — I had no track record of running a factory, yet they had faith in me."

At the beginning faith is to a small business what oxygen is to human being — without it they would shrivel up to die. However, even the most dynamic entrepreneur finds it difficult to enthuse faith into a large workforce, especially one working on the production line doing repetitive tasks. Later on if they are to expand and grow many women have come to terms with giving up part of this "personal style", learning the art of delegation and picking co-directors with backgrounds, training, contacts and skills which fill in the gaps in their own make-up.

Fear of failure

In many cases it was sheer guts and sticking power which helped these women through the early days. As one lady described it when she was poised to move from running the business as a cottage industry to a fully fledged operation, "I did think about it but I have a great determination and will. I was undaunted by the challenge. In some extraordinary way I just felt I could do it." Another woman says, "I seek out challenges. I just knew my idea would work. I couldn't see why no one else had tried."

In some ways the more extreme the challenge, the greater reserve of fighting spirit these women seem to have from which to draw inspiration, energy and driving power. Jenifer Rosenberg, widowed after just two years was left with a two year old business. "A lot of people asked me if I wanted to give up, but it was my lifeline. A lot of people thought I was going to fall flat on my face and I was determined to show everybody that I am capable and can do it and I will do it. I'm going to be an important supplier to the retail chain stores in the UK."

What's particularly interesting is that Jenifer was determined not just to survive but to achieve clearly defined and highly ambitious goals in a very competitive industry. She has succeeded in climbing the peaks she mapped out for herself during one of the toughest periods British manufacturing industry has had to face, with household names folding in depressingly large numbers throughout the early eighties.

For those women who were thrust into key managerial posts through the death of someone close to them, be it husband or father, the work seems in many ways to have served as a therapy. It was an area where they could regain their sense of control, their sense of achievement, of being master of their own fate and creators of their own future.

When asked about the psychological pressures of running a business and family, Jean Tyrell says "apart from the initial crises when my father died and this managing director who had been groomed to take over died — that was traumatic for the first few months, but after that I managed to gather people on the board and I must have been a good picker, because the people I picked have done a super job for the company, and have stayed with us."

A crisis seemed to have brought out the fighting spirit in Anne Sargent as well. Although her battle was the result of an attempted take-over when she was chairman of J&J Cash. She personally went and visited all the minority shareholders, "they were all very elderly shareholders and we went down to Eastbourne, Bexhill and all these places and we used to go all over the place to explain why they shouldn't sell and there was no reason really because they weren't doing well out of the company. It was amazing, it was just loyalty in the end. Yes, it was tough but that's what life's like isn't it. I can remember feeling sick every time the telephone went because it was nearly always bad news."

Anne, with the help of expert advice from merchant bankers, Brown Shipley, stuck to her guns. "As a result of never letting go we did win. And in the end it worked out to our advantage because over the course of the next two years we became more friendly with the people who wanted to take us over and thanks to an outside chairman, established good relations and ended up with a quite considerably better deal for our shareholders."

Physical staying power

Another common denominator which emerges early on is the sheer physical staying power exhibited by these women, a factor common to successful people in fields as diverse as business, academia, literary, arts and sciences. Jennifer Loss, for example, says, "I have a lot of energy which I think I was born with. I don't have to sleep a lot." Eileen Wiggins is so bursting with energy and enthusiasm that even when seriously ill recovering in hospital from an operation she was holding court to a throng of employees just days after being under the surgeon's knife.

Elizabeth Gage stresses the need for "inner energy" and it is something which she tries to hone in on when picking her staff. Jenifer Rosenberg says she is a terrible sleeper but full of energy, "I do have sleepless nights. I sleep so little actually. When I am on holiday, then I can sleep, but now during the working time I am so hyped up that I never need an alarm call. I'm always awake at five. I've always had a lot of energy. People do say, how do you do it?, but when I slow down and stop and go on holiday I crash out completely. It's almost as if you've been wound up and you're at a pitch and adrenalin is going and suddenly you wind down and you crash."

Art of relaxation

However, Jenifer, in common with many of the women, stresses the need for relaxation, sensible eating, fresh air and exercise. Not a quartet of priorities many of today's business-men stress; although there is a more general movement towards healthy eating it is hard to detect over lunch at most City boardrooms.

Jenifer Rosenberg again, "I think it's important to be sensible in your life style, to eat sensibly, fresh air and exercise. I don't have time to go to an aerobics class but I have a dog and I make sure that I walk him."

Patricia Grant goes one stage further, she and her husband have two dogs and she takes an aerobic class three times a week. "I think you have got to have some kind of break. You've got stress building up inside you and you either start smoking or drinking or something ridiculous and so I cope with stress by doing aerobics. I'm an aerobics teacher and I take three classes a week. Although it's my hobby, it's another business now. It's called The Body Centre and I run it with another lady, a qualified teacher."

Other women find less strenuous physical pursuits as outlets for their pent-up vitality. Those with children have few problems in finding energy burning activities and many instead relax by doing things with their hands, sewing, knitting etc. Britt Allcroft, for example, does this. "I think it is one of the advantages of being a woman. That you are taught to do things with your hands. It makes it easier to switch off."

Summing it up, these women tend by normal standards to be "hyperactive" but they channelled their energy into building up their business and social lives, whether or not this includes a traditional pattern of marriage and kids. On top of that they have learned at an early stage how to cope with this surge of energy and the frequent lava of frustration which is inevitable when the rest of the world does not work at the same frenetic, souped up pace as you.

CHAPTER FIVE:
AURA OF AUTHORITY

'I've just had a nightmare — all the directors at the company board meeting were women, and I was sitting in the corner taking shorthand'

If you talk to many women employed in industry they tend to tell the same tale. Despite the undoubted advances in the last fifty years, women at work still face a credibility gap. Each woman has to prove over and over again that she has the "right stuff" to make it to senior management.

In case you think this is an exageration in the enlightened era of the eighties, the facts unfortunately speak for themselves. You don't need to be a mathematical genius to count the number of women at board level in the country's top companies. Only two per cent of all directors in the country are female.

Credibility gap

To realise how deeply ingrained these attitudes are try a little experiment for yourself. Imagine you are opening the door of a plush City boardroom, the mahogany table is neatly laid out with pens and minutes of the meeting. Around the table sit the directors. Off-stage slightly sits a person scrawling fervently into a notebook. Right, is the picture in focus. What sex were the directors? the secretary?

So when we are looking at women running businesses it is still important not to forget the years of accrued prejudice which act as lagging preventing the draughts of progress seeping into people's minds. At any moment in any day these women, who may be running businesses worth tens of millions, may still come face to face with prejudice. By now, I don't rate the other fellow's chances very highly against them, but their authority did not appear magically overnight. It was a matter in most cases of developing a tough, steely skin to cover and protect the molten flame of ambition which burned somewhere deep in the core of their psyche.

Put on a police uniform and nine out of ten people will assume you are a person of authority and stature and react accordingly. The quickest and initially simplest way to establish your authority is simply to set up a business and call yourself the boss. Trite as it may seem, the moment women can stand up and claim the position of director for themselves the rest of society has to fall in line. True, to begin with the budding female entrepreneur holds this title by proxy until she has proved her spurs in the business world, but then so any business novice.

Inner confidence

PROMOTION

In the beginning the aura of authority was based often on little more than the woman's confidence in her own ability. Later, as success came along, this itself bred confidence both inside the organisation and with suppliers, buyers and financiers outside the four walls of the particular company.

Patricia Grant, who has always been self-employed working in tandem with her husband, says, "I've never found it harder being a woman in business, I've had local comments said behind my back — 'she's a very good husband' — that sort thing, but it's just sarcasm and I don't take any notice because they don't know what's involved". She reckons it's harder for women employed in senior posts in industry, "I think women might have a harder time if they go into certain fields, like banking, or into a big organisation and it might be harder for them to get promotion. I can understand why it's harder to get promotion. People think if we promote her and give her all this training it's going to cost thousands to do that and she could leave within two or three years — I can understand them thinking that way, because even me — as a woman — I think that way when we are promoting people."

Film producer, Jean Wadlow, believes it is important to run a tight ship and for the top girl to look "one hundred per cent" all of the time. She thinks it's vital that not only are you in total control of your business but that you are perceived by your staff as being cool, unemotional and disciplined. In fact, just like an athlete honed to be at the peak of their form. She arrives in the office at eight thirty, on a typical day leaves at five thirty and then entertains clients in the evening. While at work she has no personal telephone calls, "that's another discipline" she says.

Jennifer Loss grew with the business. From 1971 when she took over as general manager at Charles Jourdan she says, "I started learning the lessons the hard way, learning how to play poker and clear up your own mistakes, cut your losses and creating a company in a framework and building a team."

Critical early days

There is one fact of life you cannot argue with, and that's the finality of death. Many women are pushed into the corporate limelight in a family business by the death of either their husband, father or a more distant relation. The early months are critical. For these women, some of whom had little or no business experience, had a relatively short period of time to put their own imprint on the business and establish their authority. Unlike women who are involved in starting businesses from scratch and can create their own flexible managerial style, women in these positions usually take over traditional businesses run on highly authoritarian lines and have to win over not only the work force, but perhaps harder, their often ambitious and more experienced co-directors.

Perhaps the classic case of a woman coming into a business with precisely zero experience and entering a relatively hostile environment, where the existing management could not see any reason why what was good enough for more than fifty years past should not serve equally well over the next fifty years, was Anne Sargent. Anne was married to a don, living in Oxford with three children aged nine, six and three when she inherited a sizeable stake in the family firm she had previously had virtually no contact with at all.

So how did Anne go about building up her credibility? "Well I don't think I did get to be credible early on, to be perfectly honest. I was accepted because I was the niece and obviously as far as the board was concerned I didn't have a controlling interest, but I had a large enough interest to make me important. As far as the work people were concerned I think they were very ambivalent about me. I was Sir Reginald's niece and the family had always been important on one hand, but on the other, I didn't know anything, I was a woman, a young woman at that, and I had pretty funny ideas."

Road to credibility

Real authority and acceptance only came later once Anne had come to grips with the high staff costs which were dragging the company into a spiral of reduced profitability and endangering its very existence. Soon after Anne took over as chairman the company was at a critical crossroads. "It was towards the end of the sixties things started to become difficult. Wage rates had gone sky high in Coventry because it was an engineering city. Cars were the great god and all the car firms were there." J&J Cash couldn't compete with the car giants on wages. Its textile business depended on selling a large volume of low value items and costing to the last penny was vital, meaning the difference between profit and red ink.

Anne realised the problem and approached someone she met in Oxford who was running a small engineering business. Despite resistance from the existing board, she asked him to look over the plant at J&J Cash. "I got somebody I knew at Oxford involved and he said unless you can do something about the numbers in the business, you won't have a business. So we decided we would put money into development."

Her Oxford contact proved a godsend, he was a physicist and redesigned the machinery which transformed the company from a labour intensive operation to a streamlined computerised plant. "In the fifties we employed around one thousand and now we employ one hundred and twenty." The greatest opposition came not from the workforce, but the higher echelons of management who didn't like "anyone disturbing things and this was a major disturbance." The people who manned the looms surprisingly responded well, "the funny thing was the people who actually worked on the looms were never a problem — they though it was all splendid. It's absolutely not true that people are very frightened of new technology. We ended up with people operating electronic gear that you wouldn't have believed — I mean women of near retirement age learning hexadecimal language — or whatever you call it — without any fuss at all."

On the management side, she found once she had broken down the initial hostility of allowing an outsider within their hallowed walls, they were half way converted. "They didn't want people inside the place — they thought they might see something that could be useful to them. Once you got people inside and started to work on it and got over it, people became very interested."

Anne had to win her spurs the hard way, by coming up with the solution to the company's swollen overheads. In doing so

won the respect of her fellow board members and the com-
y's staff. The company was able to reduce its workforce
..gely through the staff retiring and not being replaced.

Boardroom quality

Jean Tyrell also took over a traditional family firm specialising
in textiles. For her the problems of establishing authority were
rather less severe. She had worked at the company for twenty
years, been made a director seven years before being catapulted
to the top job as managing director by a series of tragic deaths
in quick succession.

For Jean one of the first tasks was to rebuild the board. Did
she have any problems being accepted by the newcomers? "I
was there first. I hired them — they all knew they were going to
work for a woman." As for the existing staff and business
contacts they too accepted Jean with relative ease. "I'd been
there a long time and they must have thought there was some
reason for it and when my father died and this other man died
they obviously found the reason for it."

Own handwriting

Jenifer Rosenberg put her foot down early on. After her
second husband had set her up in business with a factory and
small management team, she was not happy with the colour
scheme in the factory. My guess is male readers reading this
will probably react in sympathy with her husband but the point
of the anecdote is that Jennifer was determined to run things
"her way". "Even from day one I put my own handwriting on
it," says Jenifer. "I can remember we had an enormous argument. When I went to the factory and the decorators were there
I got involved with colour schemes. I said it matters very much
to me the environment people work in and it's just as easy to
paint grey as dark green, and pale grey is easier to live in."

In fact the builders apparently painted the factory the wrong
colour and Jenifer insisted they do it all over again. "The
builders did it the wrong colour and I said, this is what I want
and you're going to do it the way I want it. They all thought I
was mad — but that's me — a great attention to detail."

She sums up the incident with a broad generalisation, "I
spend a lot of time working things out and I expect people to

do what I say. My husband was obviously a great help but nevertheless I wanted to stamp my own personality on it''. In sticking to her guns with the builders she gave her staff a clear indication of the level of professionalism and attention to the minutiae which she required from them.

Two chiefs
In any small business run by two people, there are bound to be problems about whose word is final and attempts by some members of staff to play off one boss against another. These hazards are compounded when the two chiefs are husband and wife and neither has a very clear idea the start of just how they should be planning matters. Patricia Grant describes the early days when her company switched from being a freezer whole-seller to a manufacturer.

"It wasn't easy to motivate people in the beginning because everybody was rushing around trying to do jobs and we didn't know how to do it ourselves right half the time. I'd tell them to do the job one way and five minutes later my husband would go and say 'no, do it this way' and they didn't know if they were coming or going. It was just that we were trying ourselves different methods to get production''. In the early days staff turnover was high, "we couldn't afford very good conditions, we couldn't afford to pay very good wages.''

Patricia and her husband managed to make profits every year and eventually persuaded the Highlands Development Board to invest £10,000 in the company. In terms of running her company Patricia's 'road to Damascus' was rather prosaic-ally a Tokyo compressor factory. She and her husband were shopping for compressors in Japan, compressors incidentally being the motor which goes into the company's freezers, and she was overwhelmed by the discipline and organisation of the company. "We went to see their factory and they make 3,800 compressors in an eight hour shift. Of course, everything is on conveyors, including the workers. It must be pretty mono-tonous but they don't seem to complain and we saw them all in their uniforms and how they all went to their tea.''

So impressed was Patricia Grant by these Japanese workers that she decided to implement some changes back home in the Caithness factory. In came uniforms, "we thought it was nice to get our workers all smartened up; they'd look smart and feel part of a team. It's psychological too because if you're a young kid, sixteen or seventeen, and in the morning you put on your Tee shirt and jeans, you think what are you doing, getting dressed for work or play. Now if you get up and put on your uniform, your working shoes and your working clothes, then you are educating your brain before you get to work."

Putting up the barriers

One traditional means of maintaining authority is by keeping a certain distance, establishing if you like a sense of being untouchable. A complex combination of the hidden bogeyman who can see everything and will punish wrong doing with a more benign prophet figure who utters words of wisdom from on high and cannot be disturbed by mundane matters. In fact, women tend to scorn some of these tactics and use the strength of their personality, attention to detail and talk continuously about motivating people so they give their best, rather than looking for people who simply do as they say. They tend to be concerned about explaining the reason for their action and winning over their staff, rather than simply dictating how it will be. However, this patina of sweetness hides a fierce will to be obeyed, and a staunch belief that you get the best out of your staff if they understand why they are being asked to perform a certain task in a fixed way.

"I think men like to be unapproachable" says Jenifer Rosenberg, "although it depends on their personality." Although she adds, rather at a tangent, "most of the successful men that I know have always been quite approachable." Once people have established their position they acquire a layer of natural authority which can be enhanced, rather than reduced, by letting down some of the managerial barriers in a calculated way, if often unconscious way.

CHAPTER SIX:
A MATTER OF INSTINCT

'My instinct tells me you're useless'

The traditional view of the sexes describes women as creatures of instinct and men as beings of rationality. Put baldly, after years of feminism, post-feminism and new wave feminism few men would be prepared to hold their heads above the parapet and defend this view in its most explicit terms. However, the distinction remains deeply ingrained in our laws, religion and I suspect in the not-too-distant recesses of most men's minds.

Tools of decision-making

In fact, we all, men and women, use the tools of rational thinking and instinct when making decisions every day of our lives. Education and environment may alter the balance between the two poles, for example instinct is not much help in detecting a broken fuse or rationality a great asset when dealing with a perplexed child.

Now, the standard assumption adopted without much debate is that business is a matter of taking rational, planned courses of action and as such is an environment in which men, trained to think in a vertical manner, will fare best. Actually, the reality is not so clear cut. Success depends on a goodly measure of instinct backed up by meticulous strategic manoeuvring and an ability to respond to changing needs, tastes.

Frequently when we talk about risk taking, we are really saying that people who take risks play their hunches and follow their instincts. Now everyone agrees that to succeed in business you need to take risks. They usually go on to argue that women don't make natural risk takers and so QED do not shape up into leading entrepreneurs.

If you accept that taking a risk is making a decision as much on the basis of instinct than well thought out argument, then there seems no reason why women should be ruled out. In reality, it is a matter of finely tuning both your entrepreneurial instincts and ability to evolve a strategic plan. The really top class business executives combine a talent for both, whereas most people tend to veer one way rather than another.

Many of the women included in this book are basically marketing supremos and therefore tend to rely heavily on instinct, style, flair and their ability to tune into the mind, feelings and responses of consumers. However, a handful are planners, long term strategists burrowing away, etching out the lines along which their companies will travel in future.

"I believe some people are more strongly motivated than others. But everyone has their strengths and by necessity their weaknesses. You have to put together a team," says Judith Davenport. In her case, she sees her strengths in the planning, organising and defining of the company's overall long term strategy. Her former husband and co-director chips in with the marketing flair and she has recently taken on a production director to complete the trio.

Fine tuning

The interplay of rationality and instinct is illustrated in Judith's experience. Having decided to set up a smoked fish processing plant, she carefully drew up a business plan with detailed projections. Then she took a cold blooded decision to run a company with hefty borrowings, "highly geared" in the financial jargon, as money was relatively easily available. She went to the bank armed with a mound of paperwork. "I had a very fortunate bank manager — he believed in lending money against something called fish," says Judith. In fact he also believed in the ability of Judith and her team. Was his decision based on instinct or rationality? No doubt a combination. Just as Judith's own belief in the project derived from both sources.

Another example, which shows the interplay in perspective, is the case of jeweller Elizabeth Gage. Elizabeth is a highly creative artist and as we are all taught, artists and professors are absent minded, ill at ease with figures and paperwork. Well, not quite. Although instinct does play a large part in Elizabeth's decision making it is backed up by cool calculation and careful attention to the cold matters of cash flow, overheads and stock positions.

In the early days Elizabeth proved rather cautious. Apart from a starting gift to buy raw materials, "I haven't put any money into the business at all, nor have I had to borrow any money." She opened her first shop in London's fashionable Beauchamp Place, tucked away among the boutiques and restaurants within walking distance of Harrods. After four years she says, "I realised I had reached the ceiling in Beauchamp Place, that I couldn't go any higher where I was because it was tiny and also from a price point of view you couldn't be selling a bigger range of prices and goods in a very small little place hidden away."

So what happened next? "I was looking all over for premises and by chance I saw the sign outside the shop in Albemarle Street. I thought it can't be and I rang up the next morning and found it was. And that was it." In financial terms it was a huge step, heavily increasing Elizabeth's overheads, "I have great determination and will and I was undaunted by the challenge — I just felt I could do it. I knew I'd been selling well and I knew there was a demand for my goods — I just felt I could it."

For the present Elizabeth acts as her own finance director, "I do it all myself. It was really a matter of keeping a very close tab on the business, knowing when to rein in and when to let go." In short, when to take a risk and when to revert to more basic business principles. "I can't give you any formula except that I do it on an instinctive basis, I know because I'm here all the time, I know what's happening and I control and sense every aspect of the business and know exactly what's happening, so it's a feeling that comes. That's why I think that when you have a business you can't be away from it for too long — you lose that thin thread if so."

Rationalising hunches

Anne Sargent is aware that lack of formal training means she has to rely perhaps more heavily on instinct than she would with a business degree sitting on the mantelpiece. "Though one tries to consult everybody and make sure everybody has had a turn, if at the end of the day I don't agree I usually follow my instinct. You see I haven't got the sort of measured way of thinking — I've never been taught how to think. So I have to use my instinct: I do obviously also try to follow an argument because I've learnt I had to and you can't present something at a board meeting and say well my instinct tells me we've got to do this — because nobody's convinced. But in the last resort instinct has been terribly important I know. Things that I wanted to do in the old days but was never allowed to do, because other people were in charge, have turned out to be right."

In many ways instinct plays a bigger part when you are setting up a business or running a relatively small company. Prue Leith, for example, reckons a business degree from Harvard is not going to help if you are running a small business on a shoe string and can be a positive hindrance by drumming into your head that there is a "single right way" to run a business, and that's the way the major US corporations act.

Finger on the pulse

This idea of being in touch with the business and your customers, knowing the market through some invisible process of osmosis, is a recurring theme. Jenifer Rosenberg combines both an instinctive approach to middle market fashion with a finely tuned business brain. "I think I have a great eye for detail which I regard as important, my fingers are right on the pulse. If a machine catches a cold I know about it." However, she does not ignore the basic figures, "I know our cash position every week, I know what profit is made every week and our turnover every week. I can't read a balance sheet but I don't have to — I have a finance director. But I've always known that unless you are making a profit you can't inject back any money."

One area where women in common with men stick resolutely to intuition is when picking staff. Some recent research showed that the majority of British companies rely simply on the interview technique when picking staff. This seemed to send the psychologist into a blue funk. Nothing they argued could be less scientific than basing such a vital decision on a head-to-head interview lasting at most an hour and frequently less. The idea that picking staff was a matter which could be reduced to a rigid scientific formula was taken for granted by these psychologists who had produced an array of tests, expensive naturally, which they recommend potential employees should be asked to take.

First impressions

Most British business people will probably have more sympathy for the rules of thumb followed by a number of the women included here. "I choose people that I have an instinct about, on the presumption that their skills are there. In this sort of business you have to choose people through their character and their approach, their honesty, quickness, intelligence and sense of creativity. Not everybody is a genius, but you need people who are able to manage and muster their own skills, and who don't need supporting from morning to night," says Jennifer Loss. As you can see, for an instinctive decision it is based on accumulating and digesting a lot of data from the applicant.

With due modesty Jean Tyrell will only say "I think I must have been lucky — that the right people came along at the right time." However, clearly she allowed her feelings about what would the right 'sort' to come into play. "I remember looking at applications from a marketing director who had a lovely manner, he was from way down in Cheltenham. I thought, I don't think he'd suit us. He'd never want to move away from home. I had a certain intuition that people who were going to work in the north didn't want to have too many luxurious ties with the south or south west."

Elizabeth Gage also relies on a quick flash to spotlight the right person to fill any vacant staff post. "I go for people who show an inner energy which I sense. I'm not always right, but basically when I've hesitated a lot I find that I've made a lot of mistakes." When choosing a design director Jenifer Rosenberg identified the key characteristics she was looking for and then chose someone she felt fitted the bill. "It had to be somebody I knew I could work with, who equally knew the marketplace, had personality, a way with her and could command a certain sense of authority. Yet when dealing with customers would show understanding of their needs."

Firm decisions

Having looked at how decisions are reached, another criticism often thrown at women is that they cannot make up their minds. Picture the popular references to women shopping for hours and unable to decide between "the blue one and the red one." Men in contrast are supposed to make quick, snap decisions, which incidentally are perhaps by divine inspiration also supposed to be rational and well thought out. In fact, decision-making follows a fairly simple rule. The longer the time you have to make a decision, the longer it will take and the more you are likely to waiver. If your desk is piled with a series of letters, suggestions or plans all of which require a decision you don't spend hours picking over the pros and cons of minor matters — not, that is, if you are going to succeed.

"I make my decisions. I don't find it difficult" says Jean Wadlow, "once I've made the decision I don't keep analysing why I've made the decision, I just get on with it."

CHAPTER SEVEN:
THE GOD SYNDROME

'Hello — God speaking'

To be a successful entrepreneur you need to be tough, self-reliant, confident and able to clear any obstacles you meet along the way. Unfortunately, these very qualities sit uneasily alongside a willingness to rely on others and by extension to pay for advice whose cash value is frequently intangible. All too often people running their own businesses suffer from what may be called the "God syndrome". In its male form it goes something like this, "Here I am working my tail off, seven days a week, twelve hours a day and just to keep my staff, my ex-wife, my current wife, her children, our children and my ex-wife's family." The female version runs, "Here I am working round the clock running the business, looking after my staff, my customers, my husband, my housekeeper, my nanny, my children, my social life, the kid's social life, the nanny's social life, the cost of the groceries and the inadequate service from the laundry."

The disease is endemic across a broad spectrum of small businesses, which can be defined as those employing under one hundred people. It is so common it is fair to say it goes with the territory. An occasional outbreak of God's syndrome does little or no harm, unless you have to listen to the outpouring. After all, unburdening your worries is good for the soul, if not the eardrums of the patient listener. However, chronic sufferers start to make crucial commercial decisions based on their feelings of superiority, brilliance and infallability.

That's where the seeds of future troubles may be sewn. A highly inflated ego, an unreasonable optimism about the breadth of your own qualities and an inability to seek and pay for outside professional help are the most visible symptoms. It's almost the flip side of the driving force which enables many entrepreneurs to succeed in the first place. It is why it takes a very special combination of talents and mental make-up to develop the full potential of a business and see the avenues which could usefully be followed.

Team approach

With twenty years business experience behind her, including a two year spell inside one of the country's largest corporations, Judith Davenport is a firm believer in the team approach. "You have to recognise your own strengths and the reverse, your own weaknesses. You have to bring in the talents you are lacking. If necessary you must give away enough of the company to make it worthwhile, which many people are reluctant to do. You have to put together a team. This 'I did it all on my own' is rubbish.''

Eileen Wiggins, Plastico's chairman agrees. Although she and her husband have run the business for nearly two decades, in their current sprint for growth they have expanded the board and taken on as a new director an accountant from one the country's larger firms. His added experience, contacts and knowledge will augment the board and open up the commercial horizons for the company.

Financial experience

For women often the most crucial component to bring onto the board is a finance director. While many more British companies are run by people with accountancy training rather than marketing backgrounds than would be the case in America, the reverse situation applies across the majority of small businesses run by women. As a rule of thumb, less women gain accountancy and business qualifications than men and those that do can earn relatively high salaries working as an employee. Most of the women running businesses today could probably not have held down a highly paid job when they started their enterprises simply because they lacked the qualifications and experience.

Jean Wadlow was fortunate when she was involved in the management buy-out of the film company which she was running. "Our chairman was very good at handling the finance side, having had experience of a very large group. I learnt a lot from him. Then we had a finance director and we've got very good financial advisers.''

Over at J&J Fashions Jenifer Rosenberg quickly learnt the basics of finance and realised when she needed additional expert help. "I've always had somebody to advise on the financial side because that isn't my strength.''

Jeweller Elizabeth Gage is pretty much a one-woman board. "I don't have co-directors. I'm not saying in the future that might not be good; I would have to find somebody who was a complement to me. I obviously want to do all the designing and that side — it's very difficult once you've been managing your own work just to leave everything else to someone else." At present, despite no formal training, she handles the financial side, relying on a combination of good old fashioned common sense and instinct. "I haven't found it difficult. There are periods when we are selling a great deal and then there are the periods which are quiet, — it's very hard to get things done when we're really busy."

Production slot

For Jean Tyrell, boss of Wakefield-based textile company Sirdar, the most difficult slot to fill was that of production director. "Maybe it's difficult in all sections of business to find a man who is equipped to be board material and at the sametime have firm technical knowledge, which is necessary to be able to instruct people under him." Technical boffins it seems rarely have the makings of directors. Well, in the words of that well known ad, Jean liked the man and bought the company. She spotted the right person to fill the vacant seat in the boardroom and eventually took over the company Hayfield where he was working.

As for the rest of the talent needed she says "If you've got tremendous knowledge of your own trade you can go out into the world and shop. I've been blessed with an excellent production director, excellent marketing director and excellent managing director, who came up from the finance side, who is a chartered accountant, but has been with the company so long that he knows what the market will bear, knows all the problems of the market and marketing."

Of course, the moment you start hiring staff or taking on directors there's bound to be the occasional mistake. This can prove particularly thorny at board level, but women have to learn to grit their teeth and remove anyone who does not fit the bill. As one lady said, "he just wasn't our sort. We just had to part company." Another ended up involved in the type of boardroom backfighting you see in programmes such as Dallas and Dynasty. "I had to go behind his back to the chairman. I took along my fellow director. It was all done while he was away. If I hadn't, the company probably would not be here today."

Outside help

The God syndrome also manifests itself when a person is picking outside advisers. There is a tendency to bring in someone you can bawl out, dominate and have running around on your behalf. However, the smaller the business, the bigger your lawyers and accountants need to be to protect you from falling prey to the large companies who often try to take advantage of their clout.

Britt Allcroft, who literally started as a woman and her typewriter says, "you need top notch professional advisers from day one. By that I mean accountants and solicitors. Remember to put everything down on paper." For many women this advice to go shopping for gold-plated solicitors and prestigious City accountants presents a host of problems. These firms tend to be run by men and used to male clients. Both partners and customers are frequently steeped in the traditions of Eton, Winchester and the City. They go to the same gentlemen's clubs, make the same jokes about their wives' shopping habits and are life-long members of that intangible but critical old boy network.

Tapping the City

For a woman, perhaps just starting in business, unfamiliar with finance and who has never stepped inside a City office, this may seem a daunting task. A whole new set of attitudes and behaviour have to be learned. You are the customer, they are providing a service, but without a balanced mix of mutual trust and self-interest the whole relationship will never get off the ground.

Several women running the largest companies in terms of staff and turnover have all had to learn the lesson of the importance of high quality advisers the hard way. Patricia Grant, for example, has recently just had to change her legal and accounting advisers. "At the start we didn't get the advice maybe we should have got from business people. They were probably used to dealing with crofts and farmers and small retail shops."

However a manufacturing company such as Norfrost, churning out six hundred freezers per day, was a different kettle of fish altogether. "They were not used to dealing with the manufacturing industry and certainly not one that was trying to sell nationally. We've since changed our accountants to one of the big ones, Ernst and Whinney."

Problems of success

Success in itself creates a whole new range of options, possibilities and additional need for financial advisers. "The moment I started doing very well I was surrounded by droves from the City. They didn't understand my business but they could tell I was doing alright. They smelt fees" said one woman. Many entrepreneurs who themselves would not dream of lifting a finger unless it was for hard cash, turn into financial virgins at the sight of a City stockbroker, who they frequently regard as leeches feeding off their profits once success is ensured.

This natural opposition can sadly sometimes lead to both sides missing out. True the stockbrokers and merchant bankers are out to earn their crust, but they can often turn the tap on relatively cheap sources of finance and open the route to expansion in a way nobody else could achieve. The hardest part seems to be getting across the message that seventy per cent of a bigger cake may be worth more than one hundred per cent of your existing business. Several women I spoke to could not see the advantages in going public. They simply felt they would be handing over their hard earned profits to outsiders in return for a smaller stake in their own company. They did not seem to realise just how difficult it is for companies which are not quoted on a recognised stock exchange to grow both quickly and into a medium to large size enterprise.

It is difficult to tell whether once they have made the huge leap and gone public women who are running companies change their attitudes and start to make full use of their financial advisers and City connections. For example, many City analysts express surprise that the Roddicks have not taken the opportunity afforded by the rapid rise in the price of Body Shop shares to go out and buy some complementary businesses.

Missed opportunities

In the height of the take-over rough and tumble which has gathered a momentum similar in pace to Haley's comet through 1985 and 1986, women entrepreneurs seem to have been relatively conspicuous by their absence. Nor have many of them taken the opportunity afforded by the launch in 1980 of the Unlisted Securities Market, the junior stock market to sell a small proportion of their shares to the public and therefore cash in on their business success.

The glib explanation would be to argue that going public involves greater risks and that women have a natural aversion to gambles on that scale. However, if you dig deeper there seems to be a host of conflicting feelings that are generated by this issue. For most small businesses there is the feeling of giving away a part of their flesh and blood. Then there is the insistence of making sure there is sufficient depth and breadth of management expertise. Many entrepreneurs object to doling out hard cash for what they regard as a City slicker. On top of this there is the feeling of losing control, being in the grip of outside forces. For women these considerations tend to be magnified. Many went into business to regain control over their working lives from men and here they are about to hand part of that power back. Then they have doubts about their ability to handle some of the new blood coming onto the board and sometimes feel they are supporting men who did not quite have the star quality to make it on their own. There is also a quite natural fear of what they regard as one of the last bastions of male chauvinism — the City. There is a reluctance to be caught up in the game of keeping institutional share-holders, pension fund managers, insurance companies etc. wined, dined and content with the company's progress.

There is no doubt that some of these fears are well founded, but the women who have gone public rarely regret it. Anita Roddick reckons she got about two million pounds worth of free advertising when Body Shop was floated on the Unlisted Securities Market. Pineapple Dance Studios' leading lady Debbie Moore became a household name when her company went public.

When circumstances force women to come into contact with leading City financial advisers they often find their fears evaporate and that a pinch of healthy scepticism does not go amiss. Anne Sargent was running her deceased uncle's Coventry textile firm when a family row in 1972 left the company vulnerable to an unwanted take-over bid. "We hadn't got a merchant bank or anything, so we got one, Brown Shipley, and we actually won." In the heat of battle feelings about potential conflicts between City hotshots and captains of industry fly out of the window.

"A takeover is a whole new ball-game. It was a fascinating thing to have got into," says Anne, who fought for her corporate life successfully. "We made a deliberate decision to involve the press on the advice of our merchant bank and they were marvellous. They made me go and visit every single shareholder and there were two hundred and fifty of them." Anne's experience points out the importance of calling in the right people at the right time. Knowing when you are facing a problem which you don't have the experience, training or perhaps time to cope with is essential. Otherwise there is a tendency to fall ever more frequently into the God Syndrome and rush vital decisions rather than delegate.

Learning to delegate

"My main fault is a tendency to rush headlong at things" admits Prue Leith candidly. It takes time and experience to work out one's shortcomings and strengths. The bigger the business grows the more important it becomes to master the art of delegation while keeping a close eye on the details. Britt Allcroft has just reached that pivotal stage in her business. "I have got to stop being the patron and start running the restaurant" she says. In the beginning she produced the film about Thomas The Tank which was the foundation of her business, went out and sold the merchandising rights, checked every single design and kept the paperwork ticking over. Now her husband has stepped in to handle the finances, deal with property acquisitions and computerising the company's administration. Britt is hiring someone who can go out and sign up the merchandising contracts and people to represent the company in foreign markets.

Jenifer Rosenberg has recently supplemented her board with a design director for the first time. "We've just got so large now that I just haven't got the time and I don't feel I am doing it well enough. I haven't got the time to devote to something which you really have to do uninterrupted. I think it will work because she will co-ordinate the ranges and she will present them to me and I will be able to give my opinion in a more objective way because I will be looking at everything afresh.''

Far too often adding a director to the board is viewed as a loss of control rather than increasing the company's potential. Both women and men suffer equally from this. It takes a great deal of confidence to be able to admit your own shortcomings and go out and supplement your boardroom with the right quality of people. For many small businesses it also involves learning a whole new range of management skills, the ability not simply to motivate paid employees but to make the best of boardroom talent.

CHAPTER EIGHT:
GROWING PAINS

'Not only do I want to join your gang, I want to be it's leader'

Businesses are alive, not static entities. Every day throws up new challeges, new problems, new tasks. If a company is not growing it tends to be losing out the race to its competitors. You cannot just stand still. It's a cut-throat world out there and as a company director you have to pitch in, highlight areas of profit and beat your rivals.

This is not the view of the world most women are brought up to accept. Judith Davenport summed it up, "little girls are taught to be peacemakers. If you qalk through a playground you will see the boys wrestling, fighting, falling on the floor, organising themselves into teams, planning their strategy, fight, opponents, adversaries, right back to cave men. The man went out on the plain to get food for his family against everybody else. Whereas women and children were not trained that way. At school they are taught to be gentle, quiet, to passify. I'm sure as females this is a wonderful thing, but in the business world you need to be competitive."

On the move

This is especially true as a company grows and you need to generate an ever increasing flow of turnover and profits. It is perhaps why many women are content with running businesses which represent an outlet for their own talents rather than moving up a gear to build a fully fledged corporate organisation which could stand on its own fleet if they walked out the door.

Jeweller Elizabeth Gage faces this conundrum. "I give a lot of thought to areas of expansion because there is only one of me and I take a very personal interest in my jewellery, the designs themselves and my clients." zone natural step for example would be to open a shop in America, since Elizabeth's designs prove so popular across the Atlantic. However, she is cautious, "If I had a shop in America I would not be able to give it that personal input, so it wouldn't be quite the same thing. I'm not certain at this point that there aren't enough outlets, for example exhibitions in various countries."

Since there are only so many designs one person can produce, two obvious routes to growth would be either to produce a mass market range or hire another designer, but again Elizabeth tends to favour caution. Her initial success with a mail order range of Zodiac rings appears to have been a one-off venture. "Possibly there might be a boutique collection, but I don't want to get into mass production because all my things are handmade. They have a lot of quality." Nor does the idea of selling someone else's designs appeal, "I wouldn't want to sell other people's work, because then I'd become a store like any other and it gets too complicated. Anyway, as long as I've got the ideas and people come to me I don't see why I should."

Price of growth

Elizabeth's experience can be contrasted with that of another highly creative woman, Britt Allcroft, who from the base of producing a film has created a large merchandising operation and has ambitions to become a leading company in the world of family entertainment. "If Disney can create a huge company on the back of Mickey Mouse, I can do it on the back of Thomas The Tank." she says.

Growth, of course, has its price. She is willing to give up what could be regarded as the artistic side of the business in order to concentrate on widening the base of her company's activities. This has meant harnessing her husband's talent in the field of property, delegating some of the selling of licences and instead concentrating on finding new characters with similar strength of appeal as Thomas The Tank which she and her team can develop together in the future.

Prue Leith has built her business empire on the foundation of her culinary skills, but also on her talent for picking creative people who could then carry on her work in the spirit she requires. While many women would have been content to run a small catering firm, Prue quickly recognised talents in her staff and spotted ways to capitalise on these. This served the dual purpose of allowing her to keep high calibre staff by giving them room to grow and enabled her to build a diversified business which was not just dependant on fashionable whims about cookery.

Now she is involved in building up the business, developing the catering side and clinching new contracts. She delegates the task of running her cookery school and restaurant to hand picked staff. Her husband, an author by profession, has also been caught up by her enthusiasm and has added a flair for buying property, which has proved useful in developing the company's asset base. Bricks and mortar carefully chosen generate a profit in their own right.

Franchise route

It is hardly surprising that Anita Roddick who runs the chain of Body Shop natural cosmetic shops with such missionary zeal was a lady whose sights were firmly set on growth. However, in the expansionist leap the husband and wife duo of Anita and Gordon Roddick have switched from being essentially retailers to manufacturers operating a franchise. The impetus to change gear came very early on. The initial success of shop number one perched down a Brighton lane next to a funeral parlour was quickly matched by a second equally profitable outlet within the first year.

The Roddicks then faced a dilemma. Shortage of capital put a natural lid on their expansion plans. It was a question of either trotting back to the bank cap in hand or finding an alternative solution. Gordon came up with the idea of franchising — that's effectively packaging the marketing formula and selling it on a fee basis to others who will run the shops for you. The franchises proved extremely successful and from that moment on Body Shop took on a different complexion. There are now more Body Shops overseas than in Britain and the Roddicks themselves have switched onto the manufacturing tack.

Only six out of a total of two hundred Body Shop retail outlets are owned by the Roddicks. Each shop now sells three hundred products, just under a quarter of which are manufactured by Body Shop itself. By 1987 the Roddicks hope to be producing 40% of their own products which explains Gordon's statement that "we are manufacturers and wholesalers. But we also need to understand retailing. Our shops give us the chance to practice our ideas in the marketplace."

Not many businesses change quite so radically in their fight for growth and it is interesting to speculate on the value of Body Shop today if it had gone down the more traditional path. The value of commercial property has risen multifold over the last decade.

Reducing unit cost

In manufacturing there is also a natural urge to expand, if only to bring down the costs of making your products and increase the profits on each sale. This creates an impetus of its own. While jeweller Elizabeth Gage can boost profits by maintaining scarcity, if her goods are sufficiently popular, if you are making a more mundane product you have to keep an eye out for competitors coming in, setting up as rivals and filching your customers. In that sort of environment arguments about whether to grow or not become academic, to survive you need to expand.

Running a business is a continual learning process — the curve is exponential, rising steeply in the early days and tapering off as you come to better understand the world you have stepped into. This facet of learning on the job often separates the kids from the grown ups. The story of Judith Davenport's first fish venture again illustrates some of the problems that emerge as the result of very early quick success.

Judith and husband Keith started importing langoustine to London and shipping scallops out to France. This two way traffic proved very successful. However, transporting scallops across the Channel in their natural state proved quite a task. So the Davenports realised one way to boost sales, reduce transport costs and produce higher profits was to process the scallops, stripping them from their shells before packing them onto the boats. By doing this they managed to increase their turnover and profitability. They became the largest sellers of scallops in Europe.

Unfortunately the sheer size of their achievement was virtually killing off their business. The scallop valley was depleted and Judith realised the next major assault would be on the mackerel market. Realising the massive capital expenditure which would be needed to develop this new market, Judith accepted an offer for her company from Imperial Group and worked for two years in the group's Ross Food division.

Judith put her two year spell with Ross Foods to good use, picking up hints on finance and distribution which supplemented the knowledge she had culled while managing the family's sprawling range of high street stores. She had a unique opportunity to bone up on the finer details in the fishing industry and emerged two years later with a fully developed strategy for her second bite at the fishing market.

In 1980 Judith, her husband and a newly hired production director set up Channel Foods, which specialised in smoking fish caught in her native Cornish waters. The company hot smokes mackerel and trout and cold smokes salmon, kippers and haddock. In order to reduce manufacturing costs they have diversified into a range of vegetarian mousses as this helps ensure their manufacturing capacity is kept at its maximum. No doubt as they continue to grow the range of products produced will increase as it is always difficult to know which one will turn out to be the outright winner.

Spurt for growth

It is not a very huge step from frozen fish to freezers, but we have to travel from the South West tip of the United Kingdom to Castletown in the north of Scotland to meet another lady, whose middle name is 'growth'. As marketing director and joint managing director of Norfrost freezers, Patricia Grant has worked literally round the clock to build up her company, which now boasts it can produce freezer chests more cheaply than the Japanese. Again, it has not been a matter of completely smooth progress, with a shortage of capital forcing the husband and wife team to sell a share of their business to raise capital and buy it back again once the profits started to materialise.

The Grants started as retailers, selling televisions, branded goods and offering a repair service. Patricia did the bookkeeping and managed the shops while her husband Alex made full use of his engineering skills. They built this business up and eventually sold out. The pair then turned their attention to the furniture business for seven years, when the itch to change horses once again surfaced. Patricia explains how it all started: "we'd been down to Devon to see this chap who was making small freezers, about two hundred a week, and it seemed such a simple operation we thought if he can do it in Devon we could do it in Castletown."

.It was slow going at first. They bought an old Nissen left over from the war from the council for just over one thousand pounds, and the first freezers rolled off the production line in

1974. Then tragedy struck. Alex's brother was killed in a car crash and left their other company, which was still involved in televisions, badly denuded of staff. They hung on to the television company for another five years until they realised the freezer business had well and truly taken off.

Adjusting your sights
So the Grants, rather like the Roddicks, switched from being retailers to manufacturers via a short flirtation with whole-selling. Patricia concentrated on buying the raw materials, training the staff and dealing with the book keeping and correspondence at night. Her husband handled the technical side. Together they taught themselves the principles of the business. Once a month Patricia would go on the road to sell the month's production of two hundred freezers.

As production grew the Grants needed to look further afield for customers. By 1978 they were manufacturing 18,000 freezers a year and they finally achieved the British Electro-technical Approvals Board standard necessary for any appliance to be considered by the various regional electricity boards.

There comes a time in any successful private business life when it has grown up to be a sufficient size and force in its particular market that it is faced with a new set of options. Jenifer Rosenberg's clothing manufacturing company was at a critical turning point in its history in 1986. "We did £19m in 1985 and we are projecting a turnover of £25m this year. We're at a crossroads because we've got three options open to us — do we stay as we are, staying private and grow, do we look at mergers or takeovers but still be in control because I wouldn't like to lose control or do we float", explains Jenifer.

There's no simple answer. "At the end of the day we have to do what is best for my husband Ian and I — not every company is the same. We believe in growing slowly from a strong base — it's terribly important because we do have hiccups, no business runs in a straight line, and if you've got a strong base when the problems come along you can cope with them". With a business every day brings a new set of conundrums, new areas for expansion and untried routes of growth. It is only later that you can identify critical turning points and judge whether the growing pains were worthwhile.

Customers control your destiny

Women who set up businesses as an alternative to being employed by someone else will quickly come up against the harsh realities of the commercial arena. In the early days they may be prepared to rush around twenty-four hours a day doing all the tasks from the most menial to the key decision making, but they soon realise running your own business may put you in control of your own working life, but your destiny remains in the hands of your customers.

All to often, women who think a business is equated with independence find themselves relying on a whole new set of people, particularly those with capital. Since women rarely have sufficient money in their own right they often have to depend on men, be they bank managers or private investors for cash. Alternatively they can go it alone, growing more slowly and settling for the route of self-financing.

Higher risk strategy

It is easy to make a virtue out of the decision to be self-financing but the women like Judith Davenport and Britt Allcroft, who opted to borrow heavily, have frequently grown the fastest. Of course this is a higher risk strategy, but it does concentrate the first bout of growing pains into a few years and imposes extra discipline which can be helpful.

"Borrowing from the bank has been an excellent discipline. It has taught me to put everything down on paper, to develop a five year plan", explains Britt Allcroft. Judith Davenport agrees, "our bank manager kept us very much on our toes. We had almost immediate success, which was a double edged sword. Now we have to accept the responsibility that we are no longer a small company. We have written a five year plan."

While it may be difficult to predict which areas of your business will take off, eventual success comes in recognising the company's strengths early and capitalising on them quickly. That means a quick spurt for growth, which is something many women still find hard to accept. In many ways it is a similar process to educating and bringing up a child. There comes a time when you have to let go the reins. Of course, in a business the directors will still control the overall strategy but many women entrepreneurs seem to pour so much emotion into their businesses, talking about them in terms more suited to families than organisations, that they have difficulty in really pushing their companies into the big league.

This is not just a characteristic of women entrepreneurs, some men who run small businesses also suffer from this inability to make the leap into the top ranks. Often the bigger you are, the larger the target you present to those outside wishing to take pot shots at you. As one woman said, "I don't want to be hyped. I don't want to be sold on the basis of expectations I am unlikely to fulfill." Not a phrase you would be likely to hear perhaps from a man. Women still have to learn the lesson, it seems, of being sufficiently hard skinned to understand that criticism from others is a natural result of success. They cannot expect to please everyone, all of the time and that goes for shareholders, fellow directors and even City institutions.

CHAPTER NINE:
WHITE HEAT OF TECHNOLOGY

'Keep an eye on Benson and Smithers Margery — they can become devious and manipulative if not programmed correctly'

While female scientists may not have been in the forefront of the technological revolution it has often ironically been women who have benefited from its fruits. The average kitchen today is a cornucopia of technological treats, the microchip has well and truly invaded our homes and helped reduce the tedium, drudgery and sheer physical strain involved in house-work. In factories too, many women working in the food and clothing industry have benefitted from what may be called the second industrial revolution.

Technological buzz

It is therefore hardly surprising to find women entrepreneurs among the leaders when it comes to introducing new machinery and methods into the workplace. What is perhaps a little strange to some ears is to hear them wax lyrical about the capabilities of their machines in terms we are more used to women using when describing their clothes, homes or jewellery. It is quite clear that, to use a current expression, they get a "buzz" out of installing the new technology.

In the last decade the textile industry in Britain has been decimated by foreign competition. The combination of high wage costs here at home in the late seventies, archaic, out-of-date machinery and lack of investment have been the deadly symptoms which have killed off many of our traditional companies. Those that survived have been ones with clear sighted managers willing and able to come to grips with the problems of high overheads, overstaffing and outmoded equipment.

Uncompromising course

Perhaps the classic example of this dilemma, and proof of how by taking a tough uncompromising course it can be overcome, is the case of J&J Cash, the Coventry based textile company set up in 1846. It was a family business and the entrepreneurial spirit coursed swiftly through the blood of the first few generations. Originally it formed part of the flourishing ribbon business in Victorian Coventry, but in 1860 the Gladstone Free Trade Bill trimmed the profit in that particular line. The company survived by diversifying into other products. They created a new sort of frilling with a draw string which could be loosened for easy ironing. Then there were highly decorative woven ribbons, known as jacquards. The business prospered and a New York office, the ultimate seal of profitability, was opened in the 1890's.

As the twentieth century dawned J&J Cash spotted another avenue for their textile talents and about the turn of the century moved into textile labelling and nametapes. The business chugged along in this way, still housed in some of those old Victorian buildings, for another sixty-five years before the untimely death of the company's chairman in 1965.

Housewife, mother of two young children and based in Oxford, Anne Sargent nevertheless decided after inheriting a stake in J&J Cash in 1959 that she would take an active interest in the company's affairs. She could hardly have realised at the time just how active that interest would turn out to be. She took over as chairman and for the first time started having a real impact on the company's fortunes.

Anne did not have an easy ride. She quickly had to face up to the fact that what might have started as a passing aquaintance, had turned into an old dear friend — and a sick one at that. The company was suffering from the usual range of ills which beset many such relatively small textile firms where profit margins at the best of times are small and where high labour costs had virtually made the business untenable.

Anne summed up the problem, "unless you can operate enormously efficiently and cut your labour costs, which at the time were horrific, it just wasn't on." Matters had not been improved by the past management's strategy of buying out the competition. "If you've a small company, you've very little in the way of funds — the funds had been invested in buying up old ribbon companies in Coventry with old machinery, which we didn't really want anyway."

Anne set about solving the company's problems by calling in a physicist, who she had first met through her circle of academic friends at Oxford, where her husband was an economics don. The physicist took one look at the jacquard machines and quickly saw how they could be updated and computerised. The transformation at £90,000 was no snip, that's roughly equal to over £5m in today's money, but Anne borrowed part of the money from the bank. The change truly revolutionised the company. The card room where the imprints for the name-tapes were made and processed used to employ eighty people, with the new machinery in place only one person was needed.

Technological imperative

The move towards high tech did not stop there, Anne explains, "the next stage was getting a computer — we had an ICL mainframe to start with and updated that, then had another one which we got second hand for about a fraction of the cost. Now our computer has a multi-user system which is on-line. All the ordering, processing, sorting of the orders, actual manufacture and everything is done via these computers. That whole side of the business has been revolutionised."

The victory proved temporary. By 1983 the company was once again with its back to the wall. "In 1983 overheads had got really to the state that we couldn't support the business on the old site. We'd got the new technology but we were lumbered with this enormous place to pay rates, electric charges, gas and God knows what on, and it just killed the thing." Anne, never one to sit around even when unpleasant decisions needed to be taken, realised immediate action was necessary. "I said to the chairman, we'll have to move and he said you can't move a business like that. I said I'm sure we can." True to her word, within six weeks Anne had found an alternative site and six months later the move was complete. Without Anne's ability to seize the opportunities offered by new technology and face up to tough decisions all one thousand jobs could have been lost.

Boosting profit margins

Another family run textile firm which owes its current strength to its director's foresight in introducing new machinery is Sirdar. Set up in the 1880s in Bradford to manufacture hand knitting yarn, it has managed to grow despite operating in a virtually static market for much of the last few years. The lady who has masterminded Sirdar's path over the past quarter of a century is the redoubtable Jean Tyrell.

In many ways Jean faced the same sort of problems as Anne, although on a different scale. The business she ran was also high volume, low margin. One vital decision she took was to develop her own knitting yarns. "Years ago, when we had to buy on the continent, we were dependant on seeing how the yarn would go on your supply line, and the manufacturer had nibble, then you had to give a margin to your retailers and the margin which was left at the end of the day was not all that successful. So it's better to do your own research and development, make your own yarns as far as possible, so you can get good margins and, of course, good profits."

Bradford remains the heart of Britain's textile country and the area is dappled with small yarn spinners who produce high quality products. Sirdar has achieved its sharp competitive edge by boldly investing in new technology. "There has been a big revolution in new machines and these are very, very costly. We started putting in new machines in 1970 — we were the first of the hand knitting companies to put in the new machinery and because of that we started getting improved margins from the word go."

Snowball effect

Installing the first batch of new machinery cost one million pounds and at the time the company was barely making that amount in profits. Barclays Bank proved a tremendous help. "The directors hardly slept for three months — then we had a very good year and we made over one million in profit." The new technology proved addictive, "once we got the new machinery in, we couldn't stop getting it after that — as we bought new machinery, so the margins improved — it became a snowball."

Jean thinks that an unwillingness to invest continually has been a major factor in Britain's industrial decline, "I think this is the trouble with this country, if you don't keep renewing and renewing, then you suddenly plunge in and find it's so expensive. If you have chosen the right machinery, once you get it in and running, then you find the improvements on margins are just so good, you've just got to go on getting more, which is what we've done."

Picking the right machinery is not always easy, "you see we lost all the machinery expertise in this country when we stopped making machines." That's why Jean's production director was worth his weight in profits, "it's having a super production director with boardroom experience as well as technical experience, to be able to choose which machine from which country and see which people are building and which people have the expertise that's vital," she says.

The world is now one big marketplace and all Jean's machines come from abroad, mostly Switzerland and Germany, where lower labour costs and fewer working days lost have enabled heavy industry to survive and flourish. The importance of having a technically astute board member is borne out over and over again. "Just recently we wanted a big package twister which nobody seemed to make. We went to Germany and found somebody who was doing a huge package twister, but not for our trade at all. Our production director is so clever — he goes to them and says we need a huge package twister for the fine threads and they were absolutely thrilled. They changed the gearing on the machine. It probably twisted ropes before, but they geared it to us." Sirdar now has two of these machines, 'which are fantastic — they're better than some of the machinery that was used before in our trade," says Jean. The key she argues is to have "tremendous knowledge of your own trade, so you can go out into the world and shop — get the various manufacturers to design for you without a lot of modifications."

Marketing conundrum

Of course, new machinery was not the complete answer. Unprofitable enterprises had to be closed. "We had mills in South Africa and Australia at one time, but found we couldn't equip all these new mills with the most modern machinery and it was costing us to produce, so we sold the name to Coats Paton in South Africa and Australia, and in New Zealand we have the yarn spun under licence for us. We have been able to open up in Australia with our second brand, Hayfield."

With the new machines came quite naturally higher output and it was here that Jean's own marketing strengths came to the fore. Some 12% of turnover is exports and the company made great inroads into the UK market from its lower cost base. "We went ahead to increase the market tremendously because hand knitting is a cake and there is only so much cake there. It's not expanded a tremendous amount over the last ten or fifteen years. We've expanded our share and some people have fallen out — that's the way the wind goes."

Indeed, Sirdar itself shut down two plants at home as well as closing down overseas. "We shut down a factory in South Kirby and one in Batley just to keep the Hayfield one and us here at Wakefield going. Hayfield has a similar plant to this one — all completely modern — but you can only equip so many mills with new machinery," she explains. For Jean the facts of business life are simple, "it's been survival of the fittest — people who are doing well now have had to look into new machinery and technology. As textile companies started to go to the wall, as they did in the cotton industry, they had to look into themselves and certain of the ones who didn't improve did go to the wall and others streamlined themselves, shed factories and got more modern machinery for the remaining factories."

Specialist manufacturing

Jenifer Rosenberg is also in the textile business, manufacturing clothes for the country's largest retailers such as Marks & Spencer. Although her company was only founded in the early seventies, she too had to grab the thorn of technology in order to build up her business steadily and efficiently. "To be a manufacturer today has become highly technical, highly specialised and needs total commitment," says Jenifer. "The clothing industry has changed dramatically in the last five years. People weren't investing but in the last five years, with all the new changes you had to invest just to stay in business."

In 1985 the company spent two million pounds installing a computerised cutting centre and refurbishing its factories. The advantages fed through quickly, "you can see the benefit if you take the computerised cutting. As we had grown we had four separate cutting rooms, but the cutting was not being done in the most economical way, so it was right to streamline it."

In the past the whole process of measuring up patterns of various sizes and laying them on fabric was done manually, now it's machine operated. Apart from saving time, money and labour costs, this has reduced fabric wastage to less than 5%. "It's difficult to quantify the savings, but they have been enormous. One really has to see it to imagine what it's like.

You lay fabric up on each table and this computer head goes from table to table — it moves. It's just incredibly time saving and so efficient.''

New technology and the technical skill to develop machinery best suited to their needs have together been major contributors to the success of freezer manufacturers Norfrost. The company shops around the world for its components, buying the compressor from Japan. If they can't find anything suitable, then Patricia's husband, Alex, sets about solving the problem himself. Patricia explains, "my husband is the engineer in the company. He designs machines to make machines in a lot of cases. In some instances it's so much cheaper to make a machine to do a job rather than to go into the market and buy a machine. So we often make our own machines.'' That said the company has not stinted on investment over the years, pouring back over five million pounds into new machinery and buildings.

So the idea that women and machines don't mix is not borne out by the facts. True, women may not spend hours fiddling with their latest computer toy, but that is largely because they regard them as functional rather than recreational. Women have always been aware that in an age when brute strength is coming to be increasingly replaced by keyboard dexterity, their relative physical weakness diminishes in importance. Nor are they reluctant to embrace change. You only have to look at the array of gadgets, food processors and equipment in most homes to realise that women have been weaned on the idea that the latest new fangled piece of machinery will revolutionise their lives. The reality may not have matched the advertising hype but the message has sunk in.

CHAPTER TEN:
TWENTY-FIVE HOUR DAY

'The children are at home looking after my husband'

Why slave away for an employer for eight hours a day, five day a week when you could work for yourself and control your own destiny. Many people who opt to be their own bosses are in for a rude awakening. At least in the early years they usually find themselves working round the clock, often for lower wages than before and with the additional responsibilty of employing others. Even Anita Roddick, self-made millionairess, works the kind of hours which would have the average union official sprinting to a tribunal and seeking to curb.

Self-discipline

So how do these women manage to cope? The two keys to success inside the four walls of the office are self-discipline and excellent staff. In business you can only plan so much, as Elizabeth Gage, designer and entrepreneur, explains, "I start at about nine thirty in the morning and I see my manufacturing co-ordinator for about an hour or so. I just deal with different things as they come up, but if there are certain things that I have to get done, then I deal with them straight away, but if not I do designing when I can — I find I do design best under pressure."

Patricia Grant, like many people running medium sized businesses, is involved across a broad range of areas, "I don't go in with the idea that my day is mapped out, because if a crisis arises you have to be on the spot and have to cope with that. I have my jobs, speaking to the customers, dealing with suppliers. When the customers are flying up to see me, maybe I'll have lunch with them. I also have to look after the office staff, check with the accountants as regards stock control. I look after the buying and the work of the office staff and production staff very closely, and the factory manager, so that keeps me pretty busy, just checking what they're doing and also doing it myself in some cases and seeing if their answers are the same as mine."

In many ways the smaller the company the more complex the task of running it. Tasks tend not to be so clearly defined and the boss is much more a figure who rolls up her sleeves and gets stuck in rather than a lofty, almost disembodied presence who lives on the upper floors and dispenses memos from on high.

With so much pressure just to keep the business running, there is often a tendency not to leave sufficient time to planning overall strategy.

Secretarial buffer

It is here that a good secretary is vital, protecting her boss from unnecessary interruptions, filtering through the right people and giving access at appropriate times. As women are traditionally in charge of the family's social arrangements some female bosses get their secretaries to help out on this score, especially when their social and business life overlap considerably as is frequently the case.

Jenifer Rosenberg swears by her secretary, "I couldn't function without my secretary — she really organises my life. I do a lot of charity work, have a busy social life and I couldn't do it all without her. If she sees I've got a wedding or a dinner party to go to then she takes care of the flowers or presents — it's fantastic because I haven't got time to do it."

This leaves Jenifer the time to manage her company in a more relaxed, friendly open style. "Well, everybody calls me Jenifer, which I like, they don't think 'oh my goodness this is Jenifer Rosenberg the tycoon'. Say somebody asks for me and it's someone who wouldn't normally speak to me, if I can I always find out what it is — I never think I'm too important."

This relaxed approach hides a close attention to detail, an ability to move in and spot difficult situations as they emerge and a willingness to muscle in if events are not moving smoothly towards the correct conclusion. "I think I have a great eye for detail which I regard as important, my fingers are right on the pulse. Every Monday we have a detailed meeting. If I'm waiting for a decision I now let everybody else go through the normal channels, but if I feel we're not getting a decision I get on the phone — it can be a big or small decision. It's important for me to be on top of what's going on all the time. I've got an engaged sign which nobody takes any notice of — it's like Piccadilly Circus. I get inundated with the most crazy problems."

While her secretary will be dealing with calls like an expert fencer, Jenifer herself will be attacking problems that look set to fester. "If one of our customers is messing about with this or that colour, we're not going to be able to give them the delivery they want. At the end of the day it's about making sure you've got the garments in the store at the right time. I pick up the phone and say if we don't get an answer by a certain time we are not going to be able to get delivery to you and then we do get an answer. I don't do it on a day-to-day basis because we've got a team here who are quite capable of dealing with them. On Monday I find out because we go through every single style we're making to see exactly at what stage it's at — so that gives me an update on a weekly basis, but if there's a problem they're in and out of my office."

Rigorous timetable

Jean Wadlow's approach is rather different, she keeps to a strict daily timetable and refuses to take personal calls in the office. She lives within a few minutes walking distance from her West End office. "I wake up at six o'clock and listen to the farming programme and I listen to Radio Four News, have breakfast, probably read the Financial Times, listen to classical music and I have my personal telephone calls because I don't have that in the office — they have to ring me at home — that's another discipline." She gets into the office at eight-thirty in the morning and usually leaves at five-thirty at night. Then she goes home, has a bath, changes and starts again, either entertaining or going out with clients or perhaps having people round for drinks. She keeps up this gruelling schedule nearly every day. "I'm extremely organised in everything, right down to the final details. I even buy my clothes that way — I've two designers and one person in each boutique looking after me. I can't shop from store to store and enjoy looking around — I don't do that — I get what I want and add that to the collection and that's it."

As her social life and working life run together like two lines of a railway track it's not surprising that she employs a housekeeper who looks after her both at home and in the office. "I'm lucky — Jane does all my cleaning, shopping and laundering and she also looks after me here in the office — I have lunches here."

Women whose social life is more independant of their working lives often find it more difficult to manage. Britt Allcroft said that in the first few years something had to give and it was the couple's social life — they just didn't have time for one. Now her company is expanding and she is taking on more staff, she has started to see her friends again.

Juggling act

So much for running their office lives, but what about domestic matters. Most working women have two jobs, housewife cum super-mum and boss. Balancing the needs of both sides is virtually impossible, like walking a high wire which is being jiggled continuously. It's more difficult when you are setting up a business, because money is then usually at its tightest and time at a premium.

Jennifer Loss, who has four children and an active social life argues, "yes, I am organised — I couldn't manage otherwise. I have a lot of energy, but there are times when everything loads up a bit too much and I suppose that the one happy thing is that by the time you get to an executive position earning more money helps one get out of trouble — you can always take an extra taxi or pay for extra help to get you out of trouble if things get really tight."

She adopts a flexible approach to her working hours. "If I work in France then I start at eight and we work very long hours. In England, I can either be in the office very early or I can sort out some of my personal life, then come into the office and I tend to work very late at night when I'm in London." How did she square this with her family obligations? "I came to the conclusion that it was impossible to get home at five o'clock to see the children to bed so I might as well work as late as I wanted. I do not work at weekends if I can help it. I would rather work eighteen or twenty hours every day during the week and have my weekends to myself, which are lovely. The weekends are very busy with the children."

Spending long hours in the office during the week means Jennifer had to make careful provision for her children during her absence, "today I have a daily housekeeper who is a wonderful lady and I came to the conclusion that once my nanny had got married — she'd been a great support through the years and organised everything and taken a lot of flack from the children — that I didn't want anyone living in. The children had got older and my housekeeper comes in early in the morning and she leaves technically at five-thirty in the afternoon. I have somebody who takes over for an hour but my husband is in the house after that and my second son, so I talk to them from the office."

She is a great list writer and this helps her keep track of the various strands of her life. Of course there are some hairy times but she says, "it seems to work ninety per cent of the time. I don't mind working like a lunatic as long as I don't have a nine to five job. I think we've been very lucky, we've had good health, we're lucky with the children, it's tough being a mother, particularly as the children got into their teens you've got to be around." That said, she firmly believes the support of her husband, family and friends has actually improved her performance at work. "I do think for women who are not happily married life at work must be awfully difficult, if they don't have the balancing factor of the broader sense of life outside work."

Three helpmates
Working wives with children are usually doing three jobs, their office or factory work, housekeeping and bringing up the children. It is therefore hardly surprising that successful women who can afford to do so have three helpmates, normally female. Their secretary in the office, a housekeeper at home and if they have children at home a nanny. They have to be extremely well organised and be able to galvanise their staff with Churchillian attention to both detail and overall strategy. Split second timing is often crucial when small children cannot be left alone unattended.

The sort of detail required is shown by Jenifer Rosenberg, "I've never found a housekeeper who does not need organising — you have to programme them and I do that — it seems to work but if I wasn't organised it would be chaotic. Every Sunday I give my live-in housekeeper the itinerary for the week — the days we are in and the days we are out, and I give her the menus. Then I spend about half an hour going through it with her, I put the recipes out leave everything for her and then I spend fifteen minutes every morning going through it to make sure she's clear who's coming and what's happening.''

With all these conflicting demands, it is hardly surprising that successful women stress the need to make a small space of time for themselves. It is far too easy to slip into the trap of being both a slave to the business and their families. Anne Sargent argues, ''I have met women who say the trouble about working in a demanding job is that at the weekend you are too tired to enjoy yourself or to go out, and this is a bad thing. You've got to give yourself enough time to recover and to go out and do things other than your job or you get on a treadmill, and you are worse for it and you probably make worse decisions at work as well.''

Cultural and rural pursuits

For example, Patricia's factory closes down for six weeks a year. ''We have a week at Easter, two in the summer, one in October and we have a full two weeks at Christmas/New Year. At holiday time we keep the switchboard open with one of the girl's staying behind and we keep one lorry driver working in case anybody wants freezers and we have one maintenance man coming back to check certain things.'' This six weeks obviously gives the Grants time to unwind and plan the company's over-all strategy. Perhaps rather surprisingly they don't seem to take holidays, ''we usually go off and look at other factories or something like that'', she said.

Several of the women find more cultural activities to be a source of relaxation. Jennifer Loss, for example, reads, ''I read constantly in planes, in the train and in bed at night. I read all the time. I don't go to the theatre — you can't do every-thing. When the children have grown up, we'll go to the theatre.'' Jean Wadlow says, ''I'm not a stressful person. I take things as they come. I walk a lot. I'm very interested in the arts and opera and ballet, that's where I get my relaxation.''

More rural pursuits from fly fishing to simply walking the dog also feature among the list of ways to relax. Judith Davenport's philosophy is simple to state but difficult to live up to. "I plan my day to maximise my time, enjoy my work and effectively use my leisure time. Leisure is important. I sail, fly fish and do calligraphy." Londoner, Jenifer Rosenberg says, "I think it's important to be sensible in your life style, to eat properly, have fresh air and exercise. I have a dog and I make sure I walk him — it's important for me — it gets me outside."

Gardening is another popular pastime. Anita Roddick, Prue Leith and Anne Sargent all share a love of the countryside and messing around with plants and flowers away from the hurly burly of their City offices. Anne Sargent says, "I love gardening. I love growing things from cuttings and seeds and I've created a garden with my husband from a field and farmyard in the last seven years." She also finds using her fingers relaxing, "I do embroidery, which involves quite a lot of thought, I make some of my own clothes, cooking I enjoy and find terribly relaxing." She also tries to keep up with current affairs and is an avid reader.

For two of the women religion forms a crucial ballast in their lives, providing both support and a network of social contacts outside the work context. Judith Davenport is a committed Christian, "I am in the process of setting up a Christian businesswomen's group", she explains and her faith has helped her cope with some of the inevitable trials and tribulations she has faced over the years. Jennifer Loss gains a similar strength from her Judiasm. A founder member of the Weybridge synagogue and active in a range of charities she says religion "has been a stabilising factor in my life." Through her synagogue connections she has been able to draw on the practical and emotional assistance of a huge extended family. She goes to the synagogue every Saturday and keeps that day special as a complete break from the working week, an interval which acts both as a natural close to the previous week's activities and heralds the start of a fresh week. I put everything away in a mental drawer and then I am ready to start again on Sunday."

All the women have evolved their own particular survival plans and ways to cope with stress. That said, most successful women thrive on a high degree of activity and their stress tollerance is probably way above the average. They tend to live their lives at relatively full throttle and would probably do so even if they were not running their own businesses.

When asked about the pressures involved in combining her design work with running a business, for example, Elizabeth Gage said, "I love it. Sometimes I find that, like everybody, you have great pressures on you and you feel you can't cope and then suddenly it all falls into place. I think it's a question of priorities and organising and very strict discipline."

CHAPTER ELEVEN:
FEMININE WILES

*'I'm sorry I'm fully booked on Friday — that's the day I let
my husband think he's got a mind of his own'*

Traditionally women's vital statistics are measured in inches, men's in pound notes. The role of women in the commercial world has always been central but rather ambiguous. Put bluntly, sex sells. Combine a beautiful woman with any product and you have immediate appeal. The irony being, of course that it was packaged male fantasies which were being used to sell products largely designed and made by men to the consumer, who was nine times out of ten a woman.

Shut off from the circles of economic power, often working at home for no wages and denied the equivalent chance to further education as their male counterparts, it is hardly surprising that women developed an armoury of their own to achieve their ends. They nurtured the male fantasy of the fragile beautiful irrational creature while still managing to cope with the pain of child birth and the practicalities of bringing up children, running a household and often doing community work as well. Since they could not take direct action for themselves they resorted to manipulating those around them, hence the wheedling, nagging wife so popular among the comedians' cache of stock characters.

Twentieth century watershed

Looking back, the second World War was probably a watershed. Women went out to work, kept the factories running and could never again be totally sold on the idea that their place was in the home alone. Most of the successful female entrepreneurs included in the book were born either during the Second World War or shortly before it. They are the first generation of women to be brought up by mothers who themselves discovered they could conquer the world outside the domestic hearth.

Perhaps equally important, they lived through the swinging sixties when for a brief period of years everything seemed possible. You could solve the threat of nuclear war by wearing a flower in your hair and make a million by creating the mini skirt. It was a time when the cult of doing your own thing held sway. Youth dictated and the middle aged shed some of their social shackles and followed suit. For some of the women the atmosphere at this time had a greater impact than for others. It seemed to have been vital for both Britt Allcroft and Anita Roddick, for example. Britt was given her first break on radio as a teenager in one of the popular programmes of that time when youngsters were allowed to quiz their elders. The roots of Anita's business can be traced back to the hippie philosophy of flower power, return to nature and belief that perhaps Western civilisation and values did not hold the key to happiness.

The hyped promise of the sixties bore fruit in the stock market collapse and property crisis of the early seventies when several of these women were cutting their commercial teeth. The harsh industrial lessons of Britain's manufacturing decline were written in red ink in the first few years of the 1980s. Companies collapsed, employees were thrown onto the redundancy scrap heap and the Bank of England even had to set up a recovery ward to nurse some of the weaker companies back to health.

Survival instinct

The entrepreneurs who survived and flourished in this atmosphere tended to be a newer breed who lived life by the seat of their pants. In many ways the rough and tumble of small business created survivors. The entrepreneurs who flourished were the most street wise, not necessarily those with the longest set of academic and business credentials.

For those working in traditional industries it was a matter of taking harsh decisions, closing factories, installing new technology and reducing the number of jobs. There was no room for softness, sentiment or harking back to the good old days.

Women have always had a more highly developed sense of survival than men. Not for them the heroic leap into certain death across the battlefield. They are used to buttoning down the hatches, making do in times of hardship and biding their time. Anne Sargent, for example argues, "I think women are more realistic than men. We had some hard decisions to make. I think what I really contributed was probably the ability to get things done and not mind doing the disagreeables. Men tend to say, oh dear, that's not very nice, I'll put it at the bottom of the pile and perhaps it will go away. Nothing disagreeable ever goes away — it only gets worse."

Woman's touch

Do women run their businesses in a different way to men? The evidence is patchy and inconclusive. There is a great stress on the working environment, the staff tend to be treated in what we have come to know as a "paternalistic way" and there is a meticulous attention to keeping a tight rein on the finances. Women are used to having to win their case through words not sheer force or economic power. This seems to be reflected in their management style which is to lead by convincing others to follow and only if this fails by pulling rank.

Let's start by looking at the workplace. Perhaps the clearest example of the influence of a woman's touch is at J&J Fashions. Jenifer Rosenberg explains that on one of her first visits to her new factory, "my husband said this is a factory and I said it might be a factory to you, but this is my factory and it is reflecting me. I've got very pale grey tiles on the floor and all the woodwork is also done in grey. He said "well it doesn't matter' and I said it matters very much to me. To this day our factories are all done the same colours.

When people go in they say isn't this a bright clean factory. The floors are white. You have to clean the floors every day anyway. We have permanent cleaners in the factories going round all day long. The floors might as well be a colour you can live with." A frivolous approach you may think, but sound physchology. People respond to colour, cleanliness and brightness. They feel better, work better.

Then there's the way women treat their staff. The husband of one woman interviewed told me the following story. One of the company's staff, a woman, seemed unhappy, started coming to work late and flustered. His wife it seems took her aside and the next day she was bright, smiling and hard at work. When her husband asked what had happend to produce the change he found out his wife had arranged for the woman to be brought to work by car each day so that she could see her child off to school before leaving work. He admitted that this solution would not have occurred to him, and even if it had, he would never have followed it through.

Dissolving the barriers

One of the major problems in British industry is the "Them

and us" factor. Successful women entrepreneurs seemed to have the knack for promoting a team approach, while maintaining the ultimate sanctions which go with the boardroom territory.

Patricia Grant, who owes much of her inspiration to the Japanese, epitomises this stance, "men always think if they give workers too much background about the company or what profits we make they'll take advantage of you — I know my husband thinks like that. But if people know the facts and you give them all the facts and the way the company is going, whether it is reinvesting, why it has to reinvest, what the sales are like, they won't act irresponsibly. It's only when you try to hide things that they get suspicious."

Similarly, if Patricia isn't happy about somebody's work she tries not to simply barge down to the factory floor and yell at the culprit. "If you see anything wrong on the factory floor, instead of saying I'm going to give you a written warning, or this job is not right or you're messing me about, go up to them and say, 'can you see anything wrong in this job?, do you think you can improve it?'" Note the *we*. Of course, this approach does not always pay dividends, "it doesn't always work — nothing always works. There are some people that are not adapted to industry and they should realise it and you should realise it and they probably shouldn't be there. But you shouldn't underestimate people. You give a man his wage packet and he'll tell you what his tax should be before he opens the envelope," she says.

It's not that women can't be tough if they have to. Rather that their first automatic response is to try and conciliate, talk things through. In the end they may respond like their male colleagues but their natural strategy involves seeing the problems from their staff's point of view. This can be a weakness if not followed up by quick remedial action if necessary, but it can also be a fountain of strength improving the working atmosphere and ultimately productivity.

Fields of competition
So much for the values women are traditionally thought to articulate, but what about those male attributes. Are women competitive? Here the stock answer is negative. Men tend to dominate conversations while women barely utter a word.

Little girls are taught to lose gracefully to men. This is only one side of the coin. Women are permitted to be competitive within certain boundaries. They can compete with each other for the favours of the opposite sex and both history and literature are filled with sorties of aggressive women achieving their aims by fair means or foul.

It is a short, if not easy, step to scrub out the boundaries and redefine the field on which women can compete. There is some evidence to back up the theory that women who go to single sex schools through to their teens are more likely to succeed. Three of the twelve highflyers, Jenifer Rosenberg, Eileen Wiggins and Judith Davenport went to convents and one, Jennifer Loss, went to a girl's only school. Winning is like most habits, the more you do it, the more it becomes second nature.

Then there is the question of risk taking. Women are normally viewed as conservative, adverse to taking chances and timid. They prefer bread and butter today to the possibility of cake tomorrow. This attitude is perhaps epitomised in the car advert where an attractive woman is shown first being supportive to her husband who is planning a new business and then when she realises the financial implications, including having to give up the car, she wonders whether he isn't being a mite hasty.

There are different types of risk and the same person can adopt vastly contrasting attitudes depending on the context and people involved. Britt Allcroft is a case in point. In business she has taken huge risks, borrowed heavily and mortgaged her house. At home, with her children, she is different. "I am very protective with my children. I'm the one on holiday who tends to suggest things, like doing a certain dive, and then I can't do it. I would never go on a Big Wheel at a fair."

Women are used to taking risks in their emotional lives, but have not up till now not had the opportunity to do so in the world of commerce. To take a risk involves putting your financial security on the line and women have not usually had the commercial wherewithall to even get past the starting line, let alone see if they can win the race.

Risk takers

Once they are involved in business, successful entrepreneurs of both sexes seem psychologically to respond to risk in a different way to the majority. Their own internal drive is so strong, the will to succeed so acute that they do not weigh up the risks and rewards in what many would regard as a rational fashion. They simply know that one way or another, sooner or later they will succeed and until they do they are prepared to take whatever risks are necessary. They are determined to stretch themselves. As Jennifer Loss aptly summed it up. "As a man or a woman I would have wanted to do the very best I could — anybody you talk to who is good at any kind of career usually has this thing of being the best they can be themselves, without the arrogance of imagining for a minute that you've the best in the field — you just do the very best you can."

Unlocking your potential

Successful women entrepreneurs seem to have developed an ability to harness the different parts of their personality and activate them in varying degrees according to the situation in which they find themselves. This can mean virtually slipping into a different persona when going to work but more often is a matter of tuning up some strings and leaving other emotions untouched. Prue Leith, for example, finds this process is helped by geographic distance. She says she has two parallel lives. Her work in London and her family in the country. Jean Tyrell can in the course of half an hour switch from talking cooly about spinning machines to conversing animatedly about her youngest daughter's social life.

Perhaps this talent comes from women having to cope with many different aspects, work, family and household management. They develop a knack of switching track fluently and can keep their finger on the pulse of a seemingly chaotic set of circumstances. All of which comes in handy when running a business, which is never predictable.

The world is no longer divided into the feminine domain of home and the masculine arena of work. More and more women work alongside men. They are discovering that they too can succeed in commerce. If they run their own businesses, they can also often do it on their own terms. They are free to create working environments which more closely suit their needs rather than trying to force themselves in patterns and niches which fit men's lives. At the same time many are introducing into the workplace attitudes and values which we now regard as feminine but which the Victorians would ironically have called 'patriarchical'.

CHAPTER TWELVE:
HOW TO WIN THE
GLITTERING PRIZES

'Darling, I've decided I want to give birth — to a successful business'

Most women work for a large portion of their lives, yet relatively few come away clutching the glittering prizes of wealth, power and fame. The first and most obvious question to settle is what you want out of life. "You need an honest recognition of who you are" argues Judith Davenport, "the sort of person you really are. If you are not efficient, you are not going to become efficient. Sit down with yourself and decide what your lifeplan is, what you want from life, what you are prepared to fight for and what you are prepared to sacrifice your convictions and your family for. Then there won't be any uncertainty."

Setting your goal

This is a vital exercise for everybody, but particularly for women who tend to be groomed to fit stereotypes that may have been appropriate fifty years ago, but which are of limited value today. Many women may well decide at this stage that they do not want to pour the emotional and physical energy required into running their own businesses. Others may decide they will do so after they have brought up a family or conversely may opt to delay marriage until the business has succeeded.

Prue Leith, for example, who set up her business straight from school, deliberately waited until she was thirty five before tying the marital knot. Recent statistics on the pattern of births in this country suggest an emerging hump with many women concentrating their childbearing into their early to mid-thirties. If you are running your own business, provided it is well organised, you may actually find you can spend more time at home than if you were working for someone else. Prue Leith took four months off, enjoyed being at home and tootling around the shops. Then wham, boredom set in and she was back to work.

With that step taken, the next major decision is to define your goals. Most people achieve little in their lives because they dissipate their energy instead of deciding what it is that will make them content and then going all out to succeed. Don't be put off by well meaning friends. "In many ways it is easier to run your own company than to work in a male dominated workplace" argues Britt Allcroft, who spent her twenties working for the BBC and Southern Television.

Dash of realism

Try to be realistic about your prospects. Just because you are say a super cook does not mean you can make a living out of running a restaurant. Nor can you expect success to come immediately. It's sad but true, there are no magic wands which will turn you into an overnight financial tycoon. When you read in the papers, for example, of people who have leapt to the pinnacle of business success in record time, that frequently means ten years. So don't set yourself up to fail by trying to achieve the impossible.

Women have more choices than men, but with choice comes the responsibility for taking the course best suited to your own psychological make-up and circumstances. As Jennifer Loss admits, "women sometimes don't want to go the extra step because they want to run their families."

Inner conviction

You must also believe strongly in yourself. Prue Leith's teachers dismissed her as not particularly bright, but she set up her own business at the tender age of twenty-one and has supported herself ever since. Don't think you have to be a financial genius either, "I was hopeless at maths at school" said Britt Allcroft, "but I quite enjoy the figurework involved in the business." There's nothing like struggling to earn a crust to give you a head for pounds and pence.

This inner conviction needs to be balanced by a detached view of your own strengths and weaknesses. Jenifer Rosenberg sums it up, "I think it is most important to have a goal, to know what it is, whether it's small business or a large business, to know exactly what it is you want and what you're good at. You need to know what your strengths are so that they can be complemented and it's important to know the direction in which you want to go — so many people don't know which way they want to go."

Be prepared for the bumps

Don't expect everything to fall conveniently into your lap. Jenifer again, "once you've chosen the direction you must be aware that it won't be a smooth ride — there will be problems and hurdles to overcome and you must be determined to overcome them." This is an area where, if practice does not exactly make perfect, it takes some of the siting out of the wounds.

Get trained

There is some disagreement about whether the best training ground is getting stuck into business when you leave school or spending several years obtaining an academic or business training. Much depends upon the type of business you plan to start.

Jean Wadlow, who started as a secretary, went to night school and quickly rose to a managerial position, reckons it's a matter of taking the plunge into the business world right away, "if you really want to go into something like science then you must go to university, but I think for most people who want to run a business which is non-specialist, then they should get out there and get working. I would absolutely recommend that everybody should take a secretarial course because it opens doors for you. Start as a secretary, get to learn the business and then say to whoever you are working for, look I could do that. You can read books in the evening."

Many women regret they missed out on a formal education and believe they would have benefitted from a more disciplined approach to analysing and solving problems. Anne Sargent, for example, "I think it's a great asset to have a degree, preferably in a disciplined subject. I don't think people necessarily want to be accountants. I think they want to learn to think strategically and constructively. That's the most difficult thing I've found. I don't think women tend to think in that way, I think you've got to be taught. In fact, I'm not sure if men who are not taught think in a disciplined way — I don't know — I don't think anybody does without an education." She also recommends some training in basic marketing skills.

Jenifer Rosenberg agrees, "I think further education is important today — it has become more so in the last twenty years. If somebody is sufficiently determined and has enough drive they will be successful, but to cope with the way business is today it is much better to have a further education because it gives you a more disciplined mind." She does not minimise the value of working for a company with a good training programme but regards this as a supplement rather than an alternative to a good education. "For me Marks & Spencer gave me a most wonderful training. I learnt everything there. It was like finishing school and an apprenticeship all rolled into one, but I still think if one has the ability and opportunity to go on to further education today it is extremely important."

Judith Davenport is also a stickler for education, "you can learn from the school of knocks", she says, "but you will finish up fairly battered if you do it that way." She would thoroughly recommend business school, "it's wonderful to do English at Oxford, but it has to be of practical application as well if it is to help."

Prue Leith is not totally convinced that business school is the best background for someone going into a small business. They tend to teach you how to run IBM not the equivalent of a corner shop. She reckons practical experience will probably see you off to a better start initially and then recommends cramming up on those areas where you need extra training. She, for example trained as a cook, set up in business and then found she needed to learn about wines, so took a course.

Stick with it

Once you've started don't be fobbed off by either your boss, staff or suppliers. Don't be afraid to question the way things are run. It is often by turning old pattern on their head that new, fresh and successful ideas are created. "You've got to be prepared to dig, not to let go, to look behind things and not be fobbed off," says Anne Sargent. "Women have to get used to calling the shots, not running to help others out of a spot.

On the whole women tend to be cowed by authority. Put a man in uniform and most ladies will do what he says. Female entrepreneurs have to learn to use their own judgement when seeking advice from professionals. It is important to remember at all times that you are the boss, you are paying for their ideas and skill and if you are not satisfied, go elsewhere. Don't be put off by experts telling you it can never be done. They usually just mean no one has done it that way in the past. Finally, remember the people advising you have their own commercial interests, this may be to push up their fee bill, or increase their own level of business.

Pay particular attention to your dealings with large firms. The CBI is repeatedly criticising the industry's giants for the often cavalier way they treat small companies. True there has been a recent shift among many top industrialists' perception of small firms. They are no longer seen just as fodder but perhaps as a valuable source of additional employment and training in an era when jobs are scarce and new skills are vital.

Build a team

Then you need a good team around you and even at the start the best solicitor and accountant you can afford. You should also cultivate your bank manager. As Patricia Grant outlines, "Get a good bank manager and tell him what you are going to do. You should have done your homework properly, so, for example, you can tell him if there are certain times when you'll want a bigger overdraft. If you're going into Christmas trees you're obviously going to need finance for about nine months of the year until you can sell them at Christmas."

Cultivate your bank manager

When approaching your bank manager remember two things, one, he is also in business to make a profit and two, you are the customer and should demand the level of service you need. Banks have become much more competitive in recent years and customers have discovered the power of negotiations. It's rather a throwback from the old days when banking was done on the nod and the wink but even in the twentieth century bank managers have large areas of discretion on charges. Shop around, find out the going rate for the service you seek whether it be a loan or cashing facility. Then negotiate just as you would with any other supplier.

Know your market

Market research is another vital thing. Don't just think because you've invented an all singing, all dancing electronic mouse trap people will be queuing at your doorstep to relieve you of your stock. It's no use cutting production costs by increasing volume if you then can't sell the end result.

Develop your talents

You'll also need to decide the size of the venture you are planning. Many women have built on their domestic skills, be these cooking, knitting, child care or entertaining to create small cottage businesses. Obviously the rules about running these and level of commitment is very different from someone going into manufacturing. It's a matter of fillies for courses and goes back to knowing yourself, your strengths, weaknesses and energy quotient.

On the whole, women today tend to develop a broader range of skills than men. While men's talents are focussed on certain work qualification plus perhaps some sport and DIY, women are still expected along with their commercial skills to be, if not exactly a superwoman, at least adequate with a dustpan, microwave and nappy. These skills and qualities can all be turned into a business if you wish. "Most housewives are very good cooks, very good at sewing, very good at knitting and at amusing children — all these things are in short supply in Britain and can be put into a business if only you think about it," says Patricia.

"Women have got an awful lot of talents that men haven't got. Then men go out to work, come home saying I've been at work all day and then sit and read a newspaper or watch television — few do anything else. Some do the gardening. If you look at the average household, the wife has taken charge of the garden, the cooking, the shopping — and all that's a talent on its own. It's rather annoying really for a housewife — people tend to say she's only a housewife, but there's as much talent in that if you're doing it right."

So women not only have specific talents, but general managerial experience from juggling their responsibilities, organising their families and arranging for the smooth running of the household and often it's finances. All these talents can be harnessed to set up a business if women wish to do so and they don't need to start ventures which involve high initial capital expenditure.

The list of outlets for women's talents is huge; running creches, organising laundry services, setting up cooking classes. With more and more people enjoying longer leisure hours and a higher proportion of women working, the opportunities in both the board entertainment industry and supplying the services previously done by women in their homes, such as cooking, laundry etc are growing rapidly. These are ideal areas for women to develop into businesses.

Believe in yourself

The single most important thing is to believe in yourself. For women who are either not in paid work or earning fairly low salaries, perhaps because they are part-time, generating the fountain of perpetual self-confidence so necessary to those going it alone can be difficult. As the women in this book have shown it can be done — you don't need to be a genius with a string of degrees. Far more important is determination, resilience and the ability to survive tough times. Above all, you need to have faith in yourself and your ability to succeed. Once you do that, the rest will fall into place given time, hard work, patience and a modicum of luck.

SECTION TWO

HOW THEY MADE IT TO THE TOP

BRITT ALLCROFT

Born in Worthing and brought up by her mother and two maiden aunts, Britt studied at the local school where she passed seven GCEs. She then enrolled at Worthing College of Further Education and acquired a shorthand and typing certificate. While still a teenager, Britt launched her broadcasting career as an interviewer in a series on BBC Radio called "Let's Find Out" which allowed youngsters to grill some of the famous people of the day on topical issues.

Determined to develop a career in television, Britt initially had to settle for a job as a clerk in Worthing Library which was followed by a brief stint at a local art gallery. However, she kept her sights firmly on the black box. Her first major break came when she was just twenty-one. She landed the prestigious post of presenter cum writer at Southern Television. During this time she appeared regularly on television and presented 'Three Go Round', a teenage magazine programme.

Two years later Britt moved to the heart of British broadcasting, the BBC. This time her sights were firmly placed on a role behind the flickering screen. She wrote and directed the famous children's programme, 'Blue Peter' and devised 'Get It, Got It Good' and 'The Moon Clue Game'.

After a three year spell at the Beeb, Britt decided to return to her grass roots and Southern Television, this time as a producer. She spent the next four years working on projects such as 'Junkin', a programme starring John Junkin.

The grip of the regular monthly pay slip was starting to crumble and nine years after Britt had first marched into Southern Television she quit her latest job and went freelance. She dates the early inklings of her entrepreneurial talent to the years between 1973 and 1979. During this time she continued to produce programmes such as 'The Jimmy Young Show' (ITV), 'Keep Sakes' (BBC) and 'Dance Crazy' (Southern ITV), and ran her first commercial enterprise drawing on her television connections with well-known celebrities. She arranged a series of "Evenings with . . ." which brought the public into personal contact with television do-it-yourself experts such as gardener Percy Thrower, Ann Ladbury - dressmaker well known for her appearances on 'Houseparty', a popular ITV show of that time, Mary Morris - chef and Cherry Marshall - beauty and fashion expert and ex-head of Cherry Marshall Model Agency. She also created and organised gala charity theatre shows.

The turning point came in 1979 when Britt was asked by the Central Office of Information to produce a film about the Age of Steam. While shooting this film she met Rev. W. Awdry, author of The Railway Series, the classic stories of engine folk based round the tales of a sturdy little engine called Thomas the Tank and his pals.

Britt immediately saw the marketing potential in Thomas and his engine friends. She persuaded her husband to mortgage their house and with this money, plus a large overdraft and government loans she set about acquiring the worldwide rights to the Railway Series books from publishers, Kaye & Ward.

The next task was to translate her newly developed enthusiasm into concrete marketing opportunities. The lynchpin was a series of animated films based on a realistic portrayal of Thomas. This took two and a quarter years to put together and the first programme was broadcast on 9th October 1984.

If you ask any advertising director you will be told that television stars can sell virtually anything to the public. Britt turned Thomas into a star in his own right and then cleverly cashed in on this phenomenon by setting up a merchandising operation. Her company agreed to sell licences to manufacturers which for an up-front fee allowed them to use the Thomas the Tank image on their products for an agreed number of years. Also, vitally important, she kept final say on quality control and product design. Thomas the Tank was too vital an asset for Britt to allow the possibility of his image being diluted.

Britt has now sold the Thomas the Tank merchandising

rights to more than eighty companies, including such household names as Ladybird Books, Horrockses, Hornby Hobbies, Robin Wools, Tom Smith, Waddingtons Games, Josiah Wedgewood and Pickwick International. She also in 1986 ventured overseas for the first time and has set up a marketing operation in Australia and New Zealand.

Britt's husband, Angus Wright, joined the company in November 1985, once the enterprise was clearly destined to grow by leaps and bounds and by the end of that year turnover had reached over £1m. In the autumn of 1986 Britt left her home in Southampton which had nursed the fledgling business during its early fragile days and moved down town to a smart new office in the city centre.

For the future Britt has acquired the rights to another character, which she hopes to develop along similar lines to Thomas. There is also a hefty diversification into property as the Allcrofts are planning to develop a theme park to house Thomas and his friends. This would provide a permanent home for the character which has been the cornerstone of Britt's business to date.

JUDITH DAVENPORT

Born during the second World War in Truro, Cornwall, Judith's family was steeped in the entrepreneurial tradition. Her parent's operated a trail of high street shops specialising in a wide range of goods. The women in her family had always worked. Her mother, naturally, ran the stores alongside her father. Her grandmother was renowned for running one of the largest fishing fleets in Cornwall.

Judith, the eldest child, was educated at St Dunstan's Abbey and St Mary's convent. By her own account she was a lively noisey child who "talked too much". There wasn't much scope for women in those days. Judith didn't fancy the main options which were becoming a teacher, nurse or missionary so instead she followed in the family's commercial footsteps.

While most girls of her time would have done a secretarial course Judith opted rather unusually to go to technical college, the forerunners of polytechnics, and study for a business diploma. She emerged having passed her exams and joined the family firm, which then ran about twenty shops scattered around Devon. She married at twenty-one, had her first and only son at twenty-three, acquired the nanny who had brought her up and continued to work.

It never occurred to her not to go on working. Her husband, Keith, a commercial traveller, joined the business many years later. The family firm remained essentially an assortment of small high street shops each employing less than ten people and covering a wide range of goods from handbags, children's clothes through to hairdressing salons. It was the era before the supermarket supremos had taken over the high streets.

In 1968 Judith started to flex her commercial muscles, she developed a small wholesale company to serve the firm's retail outlets. Then a chance encounter with a couple of langoustine on a French wharf led to the birth of Capstan Foods, a fish processing company. Judith and her husband Keith were holidaying in France. It was her husband who first asked why you couldn't buy langoustine in Britain. Judith said she didn't know the answer, so he suggested they buy a few and sell the ones they didn't need. The next day Judith, who had learnt French during a six month spell on the Continent, went down to the quay and bought some. At that time Keith was the sales manager for Revlon, so using his contacts with the buyers in the top London stores he managed to sell the spare seafood to several well-known West End stores the very next day.

The langoustines started off as just a novelty. Then Judith inherited from her grandmother a trawler which was fishing for scallops and losing money. So she hit upon the idea of starting a two way traffic, exporting scallops to France and importing langoustine. She quickly realised profits could be boosted by cutting the scallops from the shells and packing more seafood into the boats. Capstan Foods was born to process the scallops.

The seafood business prospered. Judith's parents retired and she decided to gradually sell off the family's retail interests and concentrate on fishing. Although it was the trawler itself which first catapulted Judith seriously into the fishing business she soon came to the conclusion that boats per se were a disastrous investment. So she sold the trawlers and concentrated on developing the business as a small manufacturer.

In many ways she then became the victim of her own success. The company was the largest seller of scallops in Europe and the local beds were almost fished out. While looking around for other products to develop, the company received an offer from Imperial Group. Judith and Keith went to work for their new parent firm for two years.

It was the first time in her life that Judith had been employed by somebody else, but she knew it would only be temporary. Determined to learn as much as possible, Judith went to Grimsby and discovered how large corporations operate. Armed with this new knowledge and with her two years dutifully served, Judith and Keith set about building another business.

Seeing ahead has always been one of Judith's strong points. She spotted the growing new market for chilled smoked fish in the delicatessens and high street supermarkets. She knew she had the financial and administrative skills, her husband would chip in with the marketing flair, but they needed a production expert. Luckily someone with just the right qualifications turned up asking for a job. He was duly taken on to complete the trio. Together in 1980 they set up Channel Foods, based in Truro.

With twenty years of hard graft behind her, Judith and her

husband found that this time they were on to a real winner. The company quickly expanded as the market for chilled food grew and a shift in sentiment away from red meat to fish and poultry helped fuel demand. A second factory designed to smoke salmon was established in Newlyn. By 1986 staff numbers had risen from the original half dozen to one hundred and turnover had reached £3½m.

After twenty-two years of marriage Judith and Keith decided their partnership worked better in the office than at home. They divorced and Judith re-married a few years later. Her second husband, Lord Wilcox, tragically died less than one year later, leaving Judith widowed at forty-six.

The company now has three factories and is planning a fourth. A distribution unit has been added in London. In order to keep production costs down Channel Foods has diversified into vegetarian mousses. Judith is confident the market for fish will develop even more quickly over the next few years and that her company is well placed to grow with it.

ELIZABETH GAGE

The youngest of three children, Elizabeth was born in London two years before the onset of World War Two. During the war she was separated from her parents for lengthy periods and spent years convalescing after a bout of tuberculosis. As a result of the illness she didn't start school until the age of twelve.

She managed to catch up with her classmates but never had time to excel. She left school with a clutch of 'O' levels and then studied art, first at the Chelsea School of Art and then in Paris. In 1964 she took what was to be crucial step in her career and enrolled in a course of diamond mounting at Sir John Cass College. She stayed there for four years lapping up all she could about designing and producing jewellery.

During this time she started designing and making collections. One of her commissions was for no less a store than the internationally renowned Cartier in New York. This gave her work a huge boost but did not solve the problem of how and where she should sell her designs. She sold through existing shops, but found this wasn't ideal, as her product was just one of many.

She then moved to America for a while and did very well with a mail order catalogue selling a Zodiac range. In 1972 she was one of the winners of the De Beers Diamond award. Her list of clients was growing and she was on the road to building a name for her designs.

When she came back to England in 1978, she set up her company. The first step was to take a small studio in fashionable Beauchamp Place, tucked a few streets away from Knightsbridge glittering star, Harrods. She had no business experience at all and worried that people would never find her amidst the rabble of competing signs. Still she needn't have fretted. Word of mouth and loyal customers kept her business growing.

After four years she realised that business had grown as much as it ever could from Beauchamp Place. First because the shop itself was tiny and second because you couldn't sell really high priced goods from a little place hidden away. So she set about scouring Knightsbridge for new premises, but there was nothing suitable.

One evening, driving through London's Wes'

Albemarle Street, Elizabeth passed a large ground floor store with a for sale sign outside. She couldn't believe her luck, noted down the agent and rang the very next morning. That was it she snapped up the shop even though it meant boosting her overheads by about seven times. She moved in with three people and barely a year later had a staff of nine.

Elizabeth runs the business side virtually single handed. She has no executive directors to help. She designs all the jewellery as well. Most of the jewellery is produced by craftsmen who do not work on the premises, but Elizabeth herself chooses the stones which form the inspiration and basis for her designs. She does not specialise in any particular gem but enjoys finding unusual stones which people may never have seen before.

She had a stroke of good fortune shortly after moving to her new premises. Connoisseur, the art magazine, wrote a feature on Elizabeth and her work. This gave her sales a terrific boost and allowed her to expand her stock, which by its nature is expensive. The trade is seasonal which given has given her a chance to design when the shop is relatively quiet.

Her day starts at 9.30am in the morning, when she sees her manufacturing co-ordinator and goes through the most pressing items. She now has a staff of eleven in Albemarle Street, including a uniformed guard to carefully vet potential customers. Elizabeth herself rarely meets the customers anymore. She finds she designs best under pressure and usually does this squeezed between two tables. She often works at weekends and her social work is tied up with business.

Elizabeth is divorced and reckons she would never have gone into jewellery design, let alone business, if her marriage had succeeded. She always imagined her life would consist of marriage and kids, but now enjoys the career she has etched out for herself. She argues that everybody is creative and the harder you work at it, the more creative you become.

Her turnover has now almost reached £1m and Elizabeth has to consider carefully how and where to expand. She has decided against another shop in London and is not keen to move down-market. The Americans seem particularly fond of her jewellery so perhaps her next step will be to boost her marketing efforts across the Atlantic, where her talent was first recognised in the De Beers Diamond competition.

PATRICIA GRANT

The eldest girl in a family of nine Patricia, known as Pat, was born in 1944 in Stockton-on-Tees. However, it has been north of the border in Scotland where Pat has made her contribution to the business world. Her first job was an assistant in a chemist shop, but Pat quickly moved on to higher things. As a child she had always wanted to join one of the services and at seventeen she was picked for the airforce.

Three years after joining the force, Pat was working as an air traffic controller, a job which required great attention to detail and immense concentration. It was during this time that she went on holiday to Scotland with one of her girl friends in the forces. While on holiday she met her future husband, Alex Grant, who had just finished his apprenticeship as an electrical engineer. The romance blossomed into a partnership at work and at home.

Pat gave up her job with the air force and moved north to Castleford to join her husband. They decided to set up in business together and opened a small shop where light electrical goods could be repaired. Alex handled the technical side and Pat set about learning the administration and book-keeping. One of the people in the firm had previously been self-employed so he taught Pat how to handle the wages, do the accounts, prepare invoices, check customer statements and balance the till.

The electrical repair business expanded so the Grants then recruited other members of Alex's family to lend a hand. Alex's sister helped out with the book keeping and his brothers, who were also television engineers, rallied round to boost the technical team. At its peak the company had two thousand televisions on rental.

With a limited population area to serve the Grants had expanded the electrical repair and television business pretty much to its full potential. They started looking around for other lines to develop. At the very end of the sixties they hit upon the idea of going into manufacturing and producing freezers. They went down to Devon to visit a businessman who was making small freezers and turning out about two hundred a week. They thought, if he can do it, why can't we.

It proved rather easier said than done. First they had to find a site for the factory. They ended up buying an old Nissan hut left over from the war for £1,000 from the local county council. The first freezers rolled off the Norfrost production line in 1974. Just as the Grants were preparing their first consignment of freezers they heard the news that Alex's brother had been killed in a car crash. His brother was still working on the television side and this was a double blow both emotionally and financially as Alex's sister had been killed in a car crash just eighteen months before.

Alex and Pat soldiered on and kept the two businesses running in parallel for several years until they could be certain the freezer manufacturing would prove profitably. When they first started it was a matter of learning by trial and error. Everyone had to muck in, Pat taught herself to do the welding and one of the men who had worked in the television shop moved over to help out at the factory. Her husband was overseeing the technical side but as a trained TV engineer he was a bit at sea when faced with the workings of a freezer.

It was very hard to build up their distribution network. They had started doing this in a small way by buying freezers from the man in Devon and selling them on, but they had not developed the market sufficiently to cope with their production. Money was tight and they relied on school leavers and housewives to run the plant. The business turned out to be unexpectedly seasonal, so without long lines of bank credit they reluctantly had to lay off workers during the lean times and rehire later. All of which made motivating the workforce, which was Pat's job, pretty hard.

Pat used to travel South once a month to sell their supply and they got used to building up their stock through the early months of the year and selling the bulk of it by the end of September. By 1978 the company was producing 18,000 freezers per year and the next major breakthrough came when Norfrost finally won the approval of the British Electricity Board, which meant the Grants could pitch for the lucrative business from the regional electricity boards.

Since that moment production has risen steadily. The company has produced and patented a revolutionary all-plastic hinge and manufactured a chiller/freezer which can alternate between serving as a regular freezer or a drinks chiller. The

Norfrost freezer is now sold under famous brand names such as Thorn EMI, Bejam and Tricity.

Staff relations have improved considerably since those early bleak days. During 1985 the company moved into new premises on the same site. The staff and the Grants themselves worked side by side throughout the long Scottish summer evenings to help build the new factory and warehouse. Pat made her contribution as well, helping to lay concrete and driving an earth mover.

Pat reckons being a woman in business has not been a disadvantage. It's just a matter of working hard, taking quick but well thought out decisions and not trying to conquer the world overnight. Norfrost has grown at quite a pace for all that. In 1978 the company's turnover was £591,000 and it employed around forty staff. Some one hundred and twenty people now work for the company and by 1985 turnover had reached £5.9m. In 1983 the company won the Lloyds Bowmaker Industrial Achievements Award.

PRUDENCE LEITH

Cape Town, South Africa, was the birthplace of one of Britain's most famous culinary figures, Prue Leith. Her early school years were spent back in Sussex, but at the age of nine she returned to Johannesburg where she attended St Mary's school. There followed a two year stay at the University of Cape Town, while she toyed with acting, stage design and logic. The lure of Paris won out and Prue set her sights on the Sorbonne. Once firmly esconced in the French capital she quickly realised that the history of French civilisation held less charm for her than the future of modern cookery.

For the first time Prue was introduced to real home cooking. Her mother, an actress, suffered from stage fright the moment she stepped on the kitchen floor. Prue was intrigued by the careful shopping and preparation which went into even the simplest dishes. She developed a passionate interest in cooking and even tried to get a menial job at the all-male Maxims, but was turned away.

Back in England she feigned a beginner's knowledge in cookery and as a result was accepted on a Cordon Bleu advanced cookery course. She augmented her formal training with a more practical apprenticeship as a cook to a firm of solicitors in London. At the tender age of twenty-one, while still living in a bed sitter in London's Earls Court, Prue launched her own company, Leith's Good Food.

Initially she started cooking for companies in the City, their friends and a growing band of acquaintances. She would cook dinners for housewives in their homes at three pounds a time. Life in a bed sitter was not exactly conducive to running a catering business, somehow there was never enough room to prepare the food. So Prue packed her bags, pots and pans and moved to a mews cottage in Paddington.

After seven years in operation, Leith's Good Food was flourishing. Prue had a staff of five cooks, two vans to deliver food, wine and flowers to her widening circle of customers. The next stage was to open a restaurant and move her outside catering business to proper commercial premises. Prue completed both tasks in 1969. She set up Leith's Restaurant in London's North Kensington and transferred the catering operation to a converted dairy depot near the Barbican in the heart of the City.

The restaurant proved an instant success. It specialises in a short fixed price menu with dishes chosen to reflect the changes of season. It is situated in three Victorian houses and was designed by Nathan Silver, the expatriate American architect, who left the internal structure untouched and used tinted mirrors to brighten the interior. The dishes are sometimes classic favourites and occasionally more unusual. Prue is more dogmatic about what she doesn't like, than what she does. So that means no canned music, no gherkins and definitely no tomatoes cut into waterlilies.

The outside catering division has grown rapidly and apart from providing lunch fare for the City slickers, it has made Snoopy cakes for children's parties, produced food for hot air balloons tethered in Hyde Park and roasted whole sheep for May balls. Leith's is the appointed caterer to the Venice-Simplon Orient Express train, providing either elegant lunches or the more traditional calorie laden English tea.

Prue has just won her biggest catering contract to provide the food for the Queen Elizabeth II Conference Centre in London's Parliament Square. There was a hard fought battle for this contract and Prue won out by actually wheeling into the boardroom trolleys laden with a range of dishes she intended to serve if she won. The contract is worth around £2m a year, which should double the group's turnover.

The third column of the business was added in 1975 when Prue created the Leith School of Food and Wine. This is a training school for sixty-four full time students and the smart Sloane Ranger set have been queuing up to send their daughters ever since its doors first opened. The school's principal is Caroline Waldegrave but Prue herself still tastes a morsel of all the dishes prepared by the students for the final exams.

A farm in the Cotswolds was purchased in 1976 called, well you've guessed it, Leith's Farm, but the original intention of breeding ducks which could later be served to customers at the restaurant turned out to be impractical. Instead the farm supplies fresh herbs and vegetable produce for the various group companies. The final brick in the Leith edifice is a property company, Location (Kensington) Ltd, that owns or lease the group buildings and the eleven flats above the Kensington restaurant, which are reserved exclusively for the staff. With the recent rapid rise in central London property prices the group's freeholds have appreciated considerably, further boosting the cash value of the group itself.

Sandwiched somewhere between running these various businesses, Prue manages to find time to be The Guardian cookery editor and to write occasional features on restaurants, food or wine for the Sunday papers. She has also written a number of books on cooking. For five years she had the unenviable task of being a part-time member of British Railways Board, especially concerned with revamping the bars and restaurants in the main line stations.

JENNIFER LOSS

Born in London just after the outbreak of the Second World War, the oldest child of Joe Loss, the famous band leader, Jennifer went to school at one of the country's top educational establishments, St Paul's. In the early days she was attracted to the theatre and was keen to go into stage management. Her father put a stop to that by pointing out it was impossible to work nights and look after a family. Jennifer, not yet married, accepted his refusal and thought no more about it.

She was not regarded by her teachers as university material, so instead her mother dispatched the sixteen year old Jennifer to the Lycee Francais where she spent three years learning French, Spanish, German, commerce and secretarial skills. When she emerged she started looking for a job as a bilingual secretary. Her best friend, who had gone to the Sorbonne in Paris, was instrumental in getting her an interview with Charles Jourdan, the French-owned manufacturers and retailers of ladies shoes.

Jennifer landed the job at Jourdan's three weeks before Christmas Day in 1959 and has stayed with the company ever since. For her first two years she learnt the ropes, discovering how to display shoes, do the book keeping and stock control. Her first wage packed was nine pounds ten shillings. The hours were long and there was no overtime. If the company was busy Jennifer could find herself working through to one a.m. the next day.

Acutely aware of being the daughter of a popular celebrity Jennifer was determined to make her own mark and succeed in her own right. Her first step up the promotion ladder came in 1961 when she was made public relations officer. A year later she married industrial designer Robert Jankel. At twenty-five she had her first child and was promoted to wholesale manager.

Unlike most of her friends Jennifer decided to continue working. Money was tight and she had been instilled with the work ethic from her childhood in London's East End. The couple took on a nanny and moved closer to Jennifer's work. She was earning about £14 a week by this stage and paying out half this amount to the nanny.

As the wholesale manager, Jennifer was involved in plenty of travelling backward and forth across the Channel. She enjoyed the job and did not plan too far into the future. In 1971 a turn of events occurred which she could not have anticipated. She was faced with a question of survival, should she fight for her job or cave in? Jennifer found the decision difficult and it was only after consulting her husband and father that she decided to tough it out. The outcome was she took over as the firm's general manager.

In 1972 Jennifer found herself running the group's two UK shops, an import section and a wholesale division. The group's turnover in Britain was in the region of £400,000. She learned as she went along. Building up a reliable team trimming back here, expanding elsewhere. Under Jennifer's stewardship the company diversified into accessories and in 1980 introduced ready to wear clothes in the UK.

In 1974 Jennifer found her family expanding again and her career rising another notch. She had two more children in the seventies, making a total of four, and was by then the managing director of Charles Jourdan, UK. The major leap came in the eighties when Jennifer opened the group's Knightsbridge store. Today group turnover in the UK is over £8m (consolidated), apart from two Charles Jourdan stores, there is Xavier Danaud selling ladies clothes, shoes and bags plus Seducta which sells products for both men and women.

Jennifer has now spread her wings beyond the UK. IN 1984 she was asked to join the main board in Switzerland and became vice president of the international company. She was made fashion co-ordinator of the group's women's products worldwide. As a result she now spends much of her time overseas.

During her working life the fashion business has changed radically and to do her job properly Jennifer has to keep one step ahead of current trends. She sees fashion as "sociological" a demonstration of what's happening in the real world. She tries to keep in touch with today's youngsters, partly by chatting to her children's friends, because they are her customers of the future.

When she first started, children tended to follow their parent's taste in clothes. Then came the sixties revolution and the development of several looks — for youth, for grown up and ready made ranges. She sees accessories as one of the big growth pointers for the future and is confident the UK side will soon breach the £10m turnover mark.

Throughout her career Jennifer says her husband has been her strongest support. When in the early seventies he decided to start his own business Jennifer was earning enough so the couple could raise cash for Robert's business against their home. Since Robert has worked largely from home he has been on hand to help with bringing up the children. His business quickly became successful and being in a completely different field there was no element of competition.

Jennifer has an active social life and is involved in her local Jewish community. She thinks this diversity actually helps make her a better businesswoman; it gives her fresh ideas and keeps her in touch with current tastes and fads which is such a vital component in her work as a fashion co-ordinator.

ANITA RODDICK

Another World War Two baby, Anita was born in Sussex, the middle child of a vibrant Italian immigrant family. Her early years were spent in Littlehampton, her home town, where she went to St Catherine's and then on to the Maud Allen secondary modern school.

Anita initially trained as a teacher at Bath. Her subjects were English and History. Her first job was a teacher and in the long vacations she use the time to travel extensively around Europe, Israel and Polynesia. She also squeezed in a spell working for the International Labour Organisation in Geneva.

Her teaching career came to a halt after she met and married writer Gordon Roddick. Together they ran their home as a hotel. The hours were long and the reward poor. So they tried the restaurant business and created a spaghetti house in Littlehampton called Paddingtons. Again the arduous schedule left little time for a social life and the money was not that great.

In 1976 Gordon landed a contract to write about his adventures on a horseback ride from Buenos Aires to New York. Anita, who by now had two children, set herself the task of coming up with a business idea she could set up along while Gordon was travelling. She decided to open a shop selling naturally based hair, skin and body products, many based on recipes she culled during her worldwide travels.

The enterprise was called The Body Shop, a name she took from an American chain of car repairers. The next step was obtaining finance. Anita learned an early and valuable lesson, play the game according to the rules. Her bank manager in Brighton faced with a dishevelled woman jesticulating wildly accompanied by two young kids turned down her first request for a loan. She says now she is convinced he thought she was planning a massage parlour. Still, she returned duly dressed and kitted out with a written statement and some figures. Having clinched the £4,000 loan Anita was on her way. She found a small shop in one of the famous old Brighton Lanes. It was next door to a funeral parlour but Anita ignored this. Her first problem was finding someone to make up small quantities of natural cosmetics based on her own recipes. The large companies ignored her request and in desperation she turned to a herbalist. The next problem was filling the shop shelves. She only had fifteen products, so decided to stock them in various sizes. Then there was packaging. Traditionally cosmetics have been sold more on their outer coverings than their inner contents. Anita wanted to reverse this process, stressing the quality and purity of the ingredients but she also knew she couldn't afford fancy packaging. So she used cheap refillable plastic bottles and wrote the labels herself.

Her tribulations were only beginning. The shop was damp with trickles of water running down one wall. Anita in a brilliant stroke of lateral thinking created a design which incorporated the water, making it look as if it was a specially designed waterfall. The year was 1976, opening day was just twenty-four hours away when Anita was faced with another obstacle. The funeral parlour next door not surprisingly perhaps objected to the idea of having a store called The Body Shop next door. It tried to prevent her opening. Again Anita turned disaster to advantage. She contacted the local papers and whipped up a publicity campaign to support her cause. In retrospect she could not have had a more well publicised launch. Needless to say she won not only her first fight but in the process drew plenty of attention to the shop.

Anita originally thought her value for money no-nonsense products would appeal to what she called the brown rice student brigade. In fact, the solid citizens of Brighton knew a bargain when they saw one and returned enthusiastically for more of the same. Anita again faced a problem, shortage of bottles. So she developed the idea of putting the products on tap and allowing her customers to refill their own bottles.

When her husband Gordon returned saddle sore from his trans American journey is was to discover his wife well on the path to success. A second shop was added within a year and since the couple did not have access to vast sums of capital Gordon came up with the suggestion of franchising the busness. An idea which at the time was more popular in the United States than here at home. In 1977 the first franchise unit was opened in Bognor Regis and the following year the first overseas shop started trading in Sweden.

It was about this time that the emphasis of the business shifted. The roots of its success had been Anita's marketing and retail flair. She continued to develop new products, travel abroad and keep a tight eye on the layout and presentation of the goods in her franchise stores. The company itself began the slow shift to manufacturing. In 1983 with outlets as far afield as Europe, Scandinavia, Greece, Cyprus, Ireland, Canada, Australia, Finland, Hong Kong, Singapore and United Arab Emirates the company started to manufacture its own products.

By this stage the company was beginning to attract interest in the City and the couple were approached to see if they wished to float their company on the Stock Exchange's junior market, known as the Unlisted Securities Market. They held back for a while but in April 1984 amidst a huge fanfare of publicity the company was launched on the Unlisted Securities Market. The shares were originally sold for 95p each but within a year had quintupled to 480p.

The company continues to grow smartly with the major impetus now coming from overseas outlets. By the end of 1985 there were seventy-three branches of The Body Shop in the United Kingdom and one hundred and four outlets in sixteen countries worldwide. Only six outlets are owned by the Roddicks. With the company's shares soaring on the stock market its price tag has now risen to over £40m.

Anita expects the market for natural products to continue to grow and abruptly dismisses anyone who rejects her business as a "fad". Nor is she worried that some of the larger stores have started to jump on the bandwagon. The atmosphere she creates in her shop is unique and a vital part is the enthusiasm of the staff who genuinely support the ideas behind the products they sell. A difficult act to follow, she reckons.

JENIFER ROSENBERG

From post girl to tycoon, that's the remarkable rise achieved by Jenifer Rosenberg. As a girl she did not shine at her studies but her enterprising spirit emerged early on when she showed considerable acumen in running the school bazaar. Her headmistress summed it up by writing to her parents saying if Jenifer put as much effort and energy into her studies as she does into organising the school bazaar she would be a brilliant student.

The eldest child in a close family Jenifer's parents helped her map out the early stages of her career. Jenifer's first target was to become a buyer for Marks & Spencer one of the few companies which in the late fifties gave women a genuine career opportunity. She was undaunted by their attempts to suggest this might prove impossible and settled for a job in the post room with an eye to higher things.

During the next decade Jenifer worked her way up the M & S job ladder to the position she had originally sought of senior buyer. At this time M & S started buying much of their fabric in America and planning to open their first stores in Europe. Jenifer was on the European committee and travelled frequently to the United States. Along the way her first marriage was left in ruins.

After a four year stint as a senior buyer Jenifer met and married her second husband. He too was involved in the clothes business, running a manufacturing company Selincourt which supplied M & S. Jenifer's ambitions had started to surface again and when her husband suggested they go into business together she leapt at the idea. J & J Fashions, clothes manufacturers was born in January 1974. Jenifer was the first M & S buyer to leave, start her own business and then supply her old employer.

Times were hard at the start. The collapse in property prices and spread of the secondary banking crisis which marred 1974 had its effect on Jenifer's new enterprise. Overnight the bank overdraft was slashed and Jenifer was faced with a battle to survive. Their home was mortgaged and they had signed a twenty-five year lease on a building in the North East of England. Her husband's help proved invaluable in the early days but Jenifer made her mark early on. With a keen eye for detail, she even made the painters redo the factory when the walls turned out the wrong shade.

After just two years, tragedy struck. Jenifer's husband died and she was left in sole charge of the business. At a crossroad Jenifer buried her grief by hard work and was determined to prove she was capable of turning her company into a major supplier of clothes for the retail chain stores in the UK. Her success is plain to see. J&J Fashion has grown from just one factory employing a staff of seventy-four with a turnover of £757,000 in 1974 to a large manufacturer with a workforce of 1,400 and turnover which tops £20m. There are now seven factories, a computer centre and a warehouse which together occupy 172,000 square feet.

Although in retrospect it looks as if the company enjoyed fairly smooth and steady growth, it was not an easy matter. Jenifer has had to build up a management team and install new technology to keep costs down to an acceptable level. Most of the money generated by the business has been reinvested. In 1985 Jenifer opened a computerised cutting centre which cost the company a total of £2m, most of which was financed out of past profits.

The new cutting room has revolutionised the business. Let's say a store agrees to buy a certain dress. The basic pattern for that dress will usually be made up to fit a regular size twelve. In the past it would take a day to produce exact copies suitable for anyone from size twenty to size eight. Now the machine can do this job in minutes.

The same machine then goes on to automatically scan the material and calculate the most efficient way of laying the design in order to reduce the wasted fabric. This can be reduced to below 5%. Having worked out the best arrangement of the patterns on the fabric the machine itself then does the cutting. The computer nozzle is suspended over the tables laid with fabric and travels swiftly from table to table cutting out the pattern.

In the old days every single part of the process was done by hand. The irony is that the factory spanning 25,000 square feet which Jenifer bought to house the new machinery used to be owned by a large public company which made products for Marks & Spencer and which she herself visited as a storebuyer.

Jenifer ran the busines single handedly for six years after her second husband died. Then she met her third husband Ian, who owned a textile company when they were introduced by friends. They married and also merged their businesses together.

Her recipe for success is confidence, determination and organisation. She claims to be a great list maker and hates to put off doing things, even if they are unpleasant. She also reckons it's more important for a woman to believe in herself strongly than for men.

The company is poised to leap into the big league. Turnover is advancing smartly thanks to the installation of the new machinery. Projections for 1986 are £25m. Jenifer and Ian are now weighing up the options open to them. They can stay private and grow at their own pace, they can look at mergers or takeovers and finally they could go for a public flotation.

Her two favourite quotes on business are "turnover is vanity, profit is sanity" and "when the going gets tough, the tough get going."

ANNE SARGENT

Anne was born in India, the only daughter of a British colonel and his wife. However, it was Oxford's dreaming spires which were to play a key part in the first half of her life. She went to secondary school there and later married an economics don at the town's university.

Rather than go to university herself Anne was finished at the House of Citizenship school, later known as Hartwell House. At eighteen she emerged to find her first job in London as an office junior at the National Association of Boys Clubs and Mixed Clubs shere she earned three pounds a week. A two year spell there was followed by a brief period as secretary to the warden at the Adult Education College in Warwick.

When she was twenty-two Anne got married and moved to Oxford. She had three children by the time she was thirty and at that stage had no inkling of the business career she was shortly to embark upon.

In 1959 her uncle, Sir Reginald Cash, left her a sizeable shareholding in his family company J&J Cash. Sir Reginald was the last member of the Cash family and he clearly wanted someone from the next generation to continue to be associated with the firm. Anne can only think he left her shares to provide some extra financial security since a don's salary is known to be poor. Still she faced something of a conundrum. She had three children under the age of ten, the factory was based in Coventry and she knew absolutely nothing about business in general or J&J Cash in particular, having never been inside the factory gates.

The remaining directors pressed her for a decision. Was she going to sell out or stay in? Anne felt it would be wrong to dispose of the shares she had been left and was unwilling to be a sleeping partner. After discussing the matter with her husband it was agreed that Anne would spend two days a week in Coventry, staying with her parents who lived nearby and the rest of the week at her Oxford home.

J&J Cash was founded in 1846, originally to manufacture silk ribbons. Over the years it had diversified into a number of related products such as jacquard ribbons, woven textile trade lables, woven name labels, woven badges, printed labels and webbings. By the time Anne joined the company was battling

140

against high overheads including massive staff costs and outdated machines housed in some of the buildings which dated back to the middle of the nineteenth century.

Anne found it difficult to learn the business, hard as she tried. She was made a director straight away but there was a conspiracy of polite distance, so she never really came to grips with any particular area being passed from department to department. In 1965 there was a major shake-up. The chairman, who was connected to the Cash family by marriage, suddenly died and there was a crisis. The existing managing director immediately suggested he simply combine this with the post of chairman, but Anne put her foot down. Although she admits she had no idea how to be a chairman, she took over this job. She dates her influence over the firm's fortunes to this point in time.

One of her first decisions was to bring in an outside expert engineer to look over the business. The response to this move was hostile at first but the existing management soon warmed to the idea of newly designed machinery. The company had spent most of its spare cash in buying up some of its competitors so when money was needed for new investment they had to turn to the bank. Anne negotiated a £90,000 loan, large by the standard of the time, to finance new machines.

Once bitten by the new technology bug and realising how up-to-date machines could reduce cost and restore the company's diminishing margins Anne went full pelt ahead introducing mini computers and visual display units for sales and manufacturing staff.

It was not all plain sailing. During these years Anne masterminded the defeat of an unwanted bid from Jones Stroud Holdings. She personally traipsed around the countryside convincing often elderly shareholders to stick with the family and her management team. After routing Jones Stroud in such a fierce battle Anne felt she should step down as chairman. Over the next two years the companies started to build bridges which resulted in an agreed takeover at a high price.

As a result Anne found herself in what amounted to a virtual non-job. She sat around waiting and waiting for several years, often tempted to walk out the office door and slam it shut for the last time. The intervening years were not kind to J&J Cash, a rush for growth at the expense of lower returns on sales was once again placing financial strain on the company.

In 1980 Anne and the then finance director won support from the parent company and Anne was made acting managing director for six months. She's stayed for more than six years, helping to restore J&J Cash's fortunes for the second time.Her recipe for success was more new technology and to reduce the company's overheads by moving to a more compact and cheaper site. She has steadily rebuilt the company's profit margins and now has staff of just 120 compared to 1,000 in the fifties when she first became involved in the company.

JEAN TYRELL

Born in the final year of World War One Jean, the eldest child, left her native Wakefield to go to school across the border in Fife, Scotland. She put the finishing touches to her education with both language and home economics diplomas from the university of Geneva.

With the outbreak of World War Two Jean was catapulted into the family textile business, desperately trying to help her father plug the gaps left by the staff who had joined up to serve their king and country. When she joined the firm in September 1939 it was still relatively small and known by its original name Harrap Brothers. Jean's first task was to wade through the piles of complaining letters from customers who had paid five old pence for knitting patterns only to find the instructions difficult to follow.

Jean set about sorting through the complaints, answering the customers' questions and developing an embryonic customer service division. She worked round the clock frequently staying till ten at night. Since Jean could not type the process was slow and laborious as she hand wrote every reply. Always one to delegate where possible Jean soon had an assistant, one of the mill hands, and even roped in her mother.

With the pile of customers letters well under control, Jean looked around to see what else she could do. Her first thought was to oversee the production of the knitting leaflets which had caused so much of her work in the beginning. Next she suggested to her father that she be allowed to take over the advertising and public relations side of the business.

Jean generated plenty of publicity for the company by going down to London and seeing the editors of various women's magazines. If necessary the company even produced special knitting patterns to go with a particular editorial feature.

At this stage Jean did not have much to do with the actual choice of yarns or the representatives out selling in the fields. However when the company, now renamed Sirdar, which stands for leader, went public in 1953 Jean was given a seat on the board and a greater say in the sales side. Six years later she was made joint managing director when it was discovered the the existing MD had cancer.

Two and half years later found herself in sole charge. The

managing director and her father died within the space of six months. Her first task was to rebuild the board, with plenty of help from her cousin, who himself died some four years later. She enlisted the assistance of her mother and nanny in coping with her three children.

Jean steadily beefed up the company's senior management but there was always a vital piece of the jigsaw missing, a top notch production director. In fact Jean had to take over one of her competitors Hayfield in the early seventies before she was satisfied with the person holding down the job of production director. Hayfield's director Jo Stewart joined the Sirdar board and Jean dates his arrival as the starting point of the firm's push for growth.

With new management in place and a strong board Jean embarked on a costly and risky programme of installing modern machinery in their Wakefield plant. A loan from Barclays Bank proved a lifeline. Under Jeans guidance the company's first move was to invest £1m at a time when they barely made this sum in profits. The directors had a few sleepless nights but the risk paid off. In the event profit margins rose, capacity increased and the company has continued to invest heavily to this day, which is why it has one of the most modern plants in Europe.

The company has a hefty research and development budget and is currently experimenting with new dying techniques for wools, acrylics and polyesters. Sirdar is the only spinner producing the high fashion chenille yarn and it now has 19% of the domestic knitting market.

In 1981 Jean, then sixty-three stepped down as managing director while remaining chairman. She was granted the OBE in the Queen's Honours list in 1982 and made a deputy lieutenant of the county of West Yorkshire the following year. The company has rebuilt its cash position and has diversified in a modest way into the hotel and conference business by buying a share in Cedar Court Hotel.

Sirdar now employs one thousand one hundred people compared to a mere fifty in 1918. Turnover and profits have grown by leaps and bounds. When Jean took over as managing director group turnover was £2.5m and profits £313,000 for 1960. After twenty-five years under her control profits had risen to

£9.5m and turnover had scaled £36m. The new machinery has meant profit margins have doubled. Based on the highest price of its shares on the London stock market during the summer of 1986 Sirdar is worth £86m.

Jean has three daughters, the youngest is twenty-eight. Her mother proved a great help in the early days as did a nanny plus a string of extra helpers. When she first joined Sirdar the company operated on Saturday but Jean opted out using the time to organise the household. The children went to boarding school when they were ten, probably rather earlier than she would have sent them if she had not been working so hard.

Now that Jean is semi retired she spends more time with her husband, a local anaesthitist, who supported Jean throughout her career and even turned down jobs away from Wakefield so the couple could stay in Yorkshire. Most of her work now could broadly be described as public relations, although these days she is more likely to be chatting up stockbrokers and analysts than editors of the women's weeklies.

JEAN WADLOW

From typist to managing director is the stuff movies are made of but Jean has made her mark behind the camera. Early on she proved her success was due to a winning combination of hard work and natural flair. Born in Essex as the second World War was drawing to a finale Jean spent her school days in Scotland.

The eldest of two children, she developed an urge to succeed at a very tender age. She first started working at fifteen and subsequently graduated with flying colours and top speeds from Gregs College, Essex.

At school she had no particular burning ambition to follow a specific career. Her mother used to tell her she had the makings of good teacher and Jean remembers taking charge of the class occasionally. That aside, in common with many teenagers she developed a passion for the movies and Hollywood in particular.

Her first job was far away from the neon screen as a secretary to stockbrokers Daniel Costello. Being ambitious Jean took evening classes on how the stock exchange work but she realised it would be to little avail. At that time the avenues open to bright women in stockbrokers were pretty limited. So she decided to cast her net further afield into a line of business where women at least got a more even throw of the dice.

Jean kept her eyes open for a job in advertising that would give her the chance to spread her wings and leave the typewriter behind. An advertisement in The Times was the key to Jean's future success. The job opening was at Charles Barker, a leading advertising agency. Jean applied and was interviewed by one of the directors Kyrle Simond, who was later to become her business partner. Kyrle was so impressed by Jean that he immediately sent her up to the chairman who was also in the process of interviewing for a secretary.

Needless to say the chairman was equally impressed. Jean had won the opportunity she had been seeking. As secretary to the chairman she was in an ideal position to learn all about business, spot which areas were growing and map out her strategy. She also had the chance to get to know the key directors who would later on prove crucial in giving her the break she had manoeuvred so hard to get.

Within two years she had made the switch from secretary to personal assistant. As PA to the television director she discovered her ideal milieu and set about learning every aspect of the job. The sudden death of her boss left the job of television director free. Jean was still in her early twenties but determined to make her mark in the world of films. So she whizzed off a memo to the directors suggesting she be given a six month trial period to prove she could handle the job satisfactorily. The board agreed and Jean proved an instant hit.

Her work won recognition both inside Charles Barker itself and in the competitive world of international advertising. Within the organisation she was promoted to the post of associate director while still in her early twenties and the Venice Advertising Film Festival invited her to sit on the judges panel, the first woman ever asked.

In 1971 Charles Barker Group was reorganised and Jean was given the chance to head up the film company, which was then making documentaries. Still only twenty-eight but with bundles of energy, determination and plenty of shoe leather, Jean developed an extensive client list. The film company soon developed a life of its own, with only 2% of its clients coming from Charles Barker itself.

Never one to be satisfied with the status quo, Jean leapt at the opportunity when Kyrle Simond suggested they should arrange a management buy-out. This is a process in which the managers buy the businesses they have been running from the group which owns them. It has become a popular mechanism in the early eighties but was still quite rare in 1978 when Kyrle suggested it.

With Charles Barker's blessings the production company was purchased by Jean and Kyrle in 1978 and renamed Wadlow Grosvenor Productions. To begin with the company had a staff of nine, a turnover of nearly £600,000 and twenty clients. Within two years turnover was just hovering under £1m and the client list had quadrupled.

More and more business was being generated overseas and to reflect this switch the company was renamed Wadlow Grosvenor International in 1984. It now has a staff of twenty, a client list of around two hundred and turnover in 1985 was £2m.

147

Jean, who has been divorced for the past ten years, devotes most of her life to the business, working long hours and entertaining clients in the evenings. She reckons there's no half way house, arguing it is a matter of either being a career girl full time or not at all. Her recipe for success is quite simply — total dedication.

EILEEN WIGGINS

Born three years before the first shots in the Second World War were sounded Eileen's first taste of school was at a convent. During the war years she went to a series of private schools in the home counties. As the only child it was naturally assumed that Eileen would join the family business run by her father, who she was very close to. She put the finishing touches to her education at Pitman's College where she studied short-hand, typing, accounting and business administration.

At nineteen she marched into the family firm D. Green, and joined her father. The company which had been set up eight years earlier with twelve employees specialised in confectionery. When she got married Eileen's husband Derek joined the family firm and they were given the newly set up disposable division to develop. Their first product was the humble wooden cocktail stick, which to this day remains among the group's range of products.

Together Eileen and Derek built up their division until it dwarfed the rest of the company. They spotted the opportunities to move into cheap plastic disposables and Eileen developed a shrewd marketing sense.

It was not until her father became ill in 1967 that Eileen and her husband were thrust into the limelight. By this time she had two children, a son and daughter, and continued to run her home while stepping up her business activities. At the age of thirty-one Eileen became a director as did her husband.

In 1970 Eileen took full control of the business, taking on the mantle of chairman. Her husband moved up to the managing director slot. They work closely as a team to this day and their daughter has now joined the company, making her the third generation of the family to work for the firm.

When Eileen took charge the company was still relatively small. The original dozen staff had grown to thirty people. Together they were turning out about five million cutlery pieces on four old Windsor machines. Turnover was around £200,000.

Eileen is an ideas person, brimming with enthusiasm and eager to expand. Her husband is rather quieter and tends to put a brake on any of her more extreme suggestions. Together they make a marvellous team. Once Eileen was firmly in the driving seat, she set about devising a five year plan to expand the business. She was keen not only to sell to new markets but to broaden the range of products.

The company was renamed Plastico to reflect the change in emphasis in 1972 and now produces a range of 1,200 products, including plastic cutlery, meal service accessories, chef hats, frills, toothpicks and cups. New markets were explored such as airlines and hotels. Products were especially designed which had a longer life than the traditional disposable plastic spoon. These are called rotables and can be used as often as twelve times. Plastico also built up its relationship with household names such as Boots, Marks & Spencer, W.H. Smith, Wimpy and Deeko.

Together Eileen and Derek developed overseas markets. Starting with the holiday resorts of Malta, Spain and Italy and then cracking the lucrative Middle East. Plastic cutlery and dish-ware is particularly useful in countries where water is at a pre-mium. Then there was the creation of a new piece of cutlery, the spork. It was a spoon whose edge was pronged like a fork. It has become a standard item in many take-away packs.

All these ideas were boosting demand and turnover. Within the space of just two years production had doubled, four new Windsor SX machines were operating at full throttle. The company moved away from its central London birthplace to larger premises in Sutton.

Seven years later the company was once again bursting at the seams. Turnover had grown by leaps and bounds, representing one hundred and fifty million pieces. In 1985 Eileen and Derek faced the biggest financial decision they have yet encountered. The opportunity to buy the freehold of the company's new headquarters arose and together they decided to invest £1.5m in purchasing the site, refurbishing it and buying new machinery.

The fruits of this investment have already started to show. The one hundred and twenty strong workforce now churns out three hundred million pieces of plastic each year. Company's turnover is approaching £5m and Eileen is looking for a period of rapid growth.

Her latest innovation is a range of brightly coloured plastic party ware, called the Rainbow Party packs, which are sold through retailers such as W.H. Smith. Eileen is also determined to crack the hotel market where she thinks there is a huge need for disposables in guest bedrooms and bathrooms.

Despite the company's aggressive growth strategy Eileen tries to stick to her father's original philosophy, which was to work hard to get to the top, work harder when you get there and don't operate your business at arm's length. Some of the original twelve employees who started under her father are still at Plastico and she argues that everyones' contribution is important, fussing as much over the factory staff as the executives.

QUESTIONNAIRE

Do female tycoons tend to be eldest children? Are their chances of keeping a marriage together less than normal? Do they learn their business instincts round the family hearth at an early age? These are the type of questions we asked our sample of twelve women. We also canvassed their views on women in business, is it harder for the fairer sex to run a business and if so, in what areas?

On position in the family, if you added together those who were the eldest child with only children, then seven out of twelve women fell into this category of first born. Rather a high percentage figure, but partly explained by the fact that where the eldest child was a woman she was often groomed by her parents to take over the family business rather than be drawn to the role of entrepreneur through her own instincts.

As for marriage prospects, the incidence of divorce among our sample was rather higher than the national average. Five out of twelve women have been divorced, but three of these remarried. This suggests it is not so much being successful which proved the problem but the change from basically a domestic or fairly low key job to a demanding post building up a business. The all too familiar tale of one partner growing at a different pace or perhaps in a different direction from the other.

Family background seems to have been a critical determining factor. With half the women coming from families where one or both parents were self-employed. A further three women had parents who were employed at director level and therefore in a responsible position involved in making key decisions about the way the company they helped to run operated. The importance of this factor is borne out by the fact that nearly all the parents in the sample, ten out of twelve, discussed business matters at home.

Many of these women were reacting against the stereotypes provided by their mothers, only four of which work. Those whose father was self-employed and who later joined the family business seem rather to have modelled themselves on their fathers.

As to the treatment of women in business, the answers quite naturally reflected personal experience and tended to vary between self-starters who had to climb every hurdle and women who took over an existing business. Raising money was one area where more than half reckoned that overall women has a harder time then men. Half the sample also felt it was more difficult for women to handle the expansion of a business. When it came to running a business the majority of eight to four said women did not have a harder time than men.

RESULTS OF QUESTIONNAIRE

1. Oldest child   5
   Middle child   3
   Youngest child   2
   Only child   2

2. Current marital status
   Married   9
   Divorced   2
   Widowed   1

3. Parents family background
   Self-employed   6
   Employed at director level   3
   Employees   3

4. Mothers who worked
   Full time   4
   Part time   1
   Never   7

5. Female relations who worked
   Full time   5
   Part time   0
   Never   4

6. Business matters were discussed at home
   Frequently   5
   Sometimes   5
   Never   2

7. Women have a harder time than men starting a business
   True   5
   False   1
   Same   6

8. Women have a harder time than men running a business
   True   4
   False   2
   Same   6

9. Women have a harder time expanding the business than men

True	6
False	1
Same	5

10. Women have a harder time raising finance then men

True	7
False	1
Same	4

Also Available from Rosters Ltd.

500 MONEY SAVING IDEAS
Rosemary Burr, Margaret Dibben and Wendy Elkington
Price £5

The ultimate money book — three of the country's top personal finance journalists have teamed up to produce a feast of money saving ideas. Plus, inside you'll find vouchers worth up to £200, which can be used to save you money on a range of household goods, electrical equipment, dry cleaning and even holidays.

You'll find tips on cutting pounds off your shopping bills, heating costs, travel and entertainment. There's handy hints for families, the divorced, singles, retired, students and the unemployed. Plenty of pound stretching ideas to help everyone make their money go further.

INVESTORS A-Z by ROSEMARY BURR
Sponsored by Fidelity International
Price £5.99

Break through the jargon barrier and start understanding the world of money more clearly. Inside you'll find 700 terms explained in a simple and down to earth manner. If you're ever been confused by the terminology which litters most savings products, then you'll find this book an essential and friendly guide.

Includes explanations on banking, building societies, economics, general insurance, life assurance, loans, mortgages, National Savings, pensions, shares, tax and unit trusts.

THE PRUDENTIAL BOOK OF MONEY

Whether you want to build a cash sum, generate a growing income or simply maintain the real value of your savings, The Prudential Book of Money, will put you in the picture. Includes:- • strategies to beat the budgeting blues • how to earn the maximum return on your cash balances • cheapest forms of credit • getting a roof over your head • wising up to unit trusts • increasing your future income • profiting from companies around the world • protecting your family • boosting your pension • money hints for travellers

Written by Britain's top personal financial journalists, sound value for money at just £3.50.

Publication date: February 1987

THE SHARE BOOK by ROSEMARY BURR

In the 1986 Budget the government introduced a new tax free scheme to encourage small investors to buy shares. The plan will be available from January 1987. Make sure you are in a position to take full advantage of the share revolution. The Share Book, with an introduction from the Prime Minister, Margaret Thatcher, will show you how.

'For too long the world of stocks and shares has been a mystery understood by a small minority. Yet the new opportunities will go begging unless enough people know how to take advantage of them. Now, at last the tide is turning and I am sure this book will contribute to this process. It is about the nuts and bolts of buying, holding and selling shares. It should prove a valuable source of information an advice for many.' Mrs Thatcher.

'takes the mystique out of the stock market.' *The Guardian*
'full of unstiffily written information; *Observer*
'a great present for the first-time shareholder' *Sunday Express*
'a timely guide for all newcomers who are entering the fray as ordinary shareholders' *Daily Express*
'it goes right from the basics and is completely free of the type of jargon that frightens so many would-be investors' *Insurance Age*

ISBN 0 948032 10 3   Price: £5.99

FUNNY MONEY by ALAN RALPH

If you thought money was no laughing matter then this collection of cartoons by Alan Ralph, a regular contributor to The Guardian Weekend Money columns, should change your mind.

'His cartoons are sharp and often merciless . . . and frequently remind those who have control over our money that we can kick back. The cartoons rate more than a casual glance.' *The Guardian*
'If they don't make you chuckle perhaps your bank manager might see the funny side of things next time you call on him.' *The Times*
'witty one-liners' *Money Marketing*

ISBN 0 948032 00 6   Price: £2.95